Ron Schara's
Twin Cities Fishing Guide

Design/Michael Carroll
Illustrations/Cindy Gillmore

Published by the Minneapolis Tribune
Minneapolis Star & Tribune Company
425 Portland Av./Minneapolis/Minn. 55488

First printing/

Library of Congress Cataloging in Publication Data

Schara, Ron.
    Ron Schara's Twin Cities Fishing Guide.

      1. Fishing--Minnesota--Minneapolis--Guide-
books. 2. Fishing--Minnesota--St. Paul--
Guide-books. I. Title.
SH511.S3	799.1'1'097765	81-22555
		AACR2
ISBN 0-932272-08-8

Acknowledgments

A fisherman really ought not brag unless he digs his own worms.

It's a rule that also should apply to fishermen who write fishing books.

Much of the fishing information that appears in the Twin Cities Fishing Guide is not my own. It was donated by fellow anglers who long ago discovered the joys of fishing within the seven-county Twin Cities area.

Unfortunately, I don't know all their names. I met them on fishing docks, in bait shops, along river banks and in fishing boats.

By the way, some of the "fishermen" I met were women. To use a different word in these pages to describe women anglers is awkward and probably unnecessary. Unlike other sports, sexism is unknown in a fishing boat simply because the title of fisherman says more about what you do than who you are.

A few of my fishing companions deserve special mention for taking the time and the interest in wetting a line amid the masses. Wayne Ekelund and Larry Bollig generously shared their knowledge about fishing in the Twin Cities and repeatedly demonstrated their angling skills. Don Oster showed me that the excitement and drama of sport fishing—the top-water strikes, the missed lunkers, the solitude of dawn—also are available to the fisherman who never leaves the city.

The same spirit is exhibited by Duane Shodeen, metro supervisor of fisheries for the Minnesota Department of Natural Resources. Because of Shodeen and his fisheries staff, the city waters provide more angling opportunities than ever before.

And lastly, I should thank the many anglers who by their enthusiasm reminded me that the fishing sport has a common bond that does not begin or end at the city limits.

Ron Schara
March 1982

Contents

City fishing? Why not!/

Cities bustle and suburbs sprawl, but a fish remains a fish.

Call it the motto of a fisherman in a metropolis.

Fact is, there's no such thing as a farm fish or a wilderness fish or a city slicker fish. Fish simply live where they live. They can't move to the country or settle in the suburbs. If they don't like the neighborhood, they can't pack up and leave. What they swim in is what they've got.

And that's good.

The fish that swim in the waters of the seven-county Minneapolis-St. Paul metropolitan area don't know they're surrounded by freeways, stoplights and shopping centers.

The muskies of Lake Harriet never have heard the summer band concerts. The bass of Lake Calhoun are unaware of Lake Street traffic jams. And those hectic sessions of the Minnesota Legislature in St. Paul mean nothing to the bluegills of Lake Phalen.

And that's good.

They may be city fish but they act the way fish act. The waters of Lake Minnetonka may be relentlessly stirred by weekend cruisers. But under the waves there are bass willing to inhale a plastic worm. Medicine Lake may be surrounded by houses but that doesn't affect the ravenous appetite of a toothy northern pike.

And so it goes. There may be sunbathers on the beaches, waterskiers in the bays, junkyards on the river banks, noisy freeways and strip joints on Hennepin. But nothing bothers the fish.

Nor should the urban bustle bother the fisherman. In and around the Twin Cities, there are fish to be caught. Plenty of fish.

What more does an angler need to know?

Granted, city fishing takes some getting used to. Early one morning I was casting for smallmouth along the rocky banks of the Mississippi while bumper-to-bumper traffic roared overhead on the Lake Street bridge.

Take my word for it: A little horn honking and tire screeching isn't any worse than a mosquito attack in the BWCA.

Besides, a city fisherman will have experiences a wilderness angler could never match. For instance, that same morning on the river bank I found a pay telephone that had been dumped by vandals. There was nothing missing on the phone except the booth and the coin box. Such shoreline surprises help shorten the time between bites.

I learned something else that morning. There I was, surrounded by more than a million people, but there wasn't a soul on the river except my fishing partner. No warm souls anyway.

"Once in a while, if you fish here much, you'll find a cadaver," said my partner, a veteran angler of the river banks. "Never know when a snag on the river could be a body."

Fortunately, there was nothing caught but river smallmouth. And the bronze fish were doing their thing right in the city. Hitting small spinners, leaping like baby tarpon and dodging among the river rocks as smallmouth are supposed to do.

Good fishing is where you find it. In this case, the search for a tight line is where most anglers least expect it to be, the city environs.

There are some 200 fishing lakes, portions of four rivers and even a trout stream within the seven-county metropolitan area. If all the water were dumped in one spot, it would cover about 81,000 acres.

There also is fishing water, Trout-Air, where

you'll never get skunked. But you'll pay for it. Located along Interstate 35 near Forest Lake, Trout-Air offers year-around fishing in open-water ponds. You may catch whatever you can afford.

Which means that none of us—residents of the suburbs or downtown condos—is very far from a place to wet a line.

What we'll catch is another matter, of course. Fishing is a skill. As such, the city angler's bounty will vary depending on those skills. The lakes also vary in their quantity of gamefish. A number of lakes in the Twin Cities are marginal fishing waters, occasionally suffering a winter kill of fish.

Still, it's possible within the Twin Cities to catch nearly every major gamefish species available to anglers elsewhere in the state. And some lunkers, too, such as muskies, northern pike, largemouth and smallmouth bass.

Oh, I know what you're thinking. You go ''north'' when you're ''serious'' about fishing. Fine. There are qualities the north woods bring to the angling sport that can't be matched by the IDS Tower.

Keep in mind, however, that the fish of Minneapolis and St. Paul don't go away for the weekend. If the objective is to catch fish

(and it is or you wouldn't put a hook on the end of the line), the waters of the metropolis should not be overlooked.

This fishing guide to the Twin Cities is written in the spirit of aiding your search. It is also written in the belief that fishpoles and minnow buckets will enhance the lifestyle of Twin Cities residents as much as tailgate parties, Winter Carnivals and Aquatennials. For many reasons.

To catch a hefty fish within sight of the IDS Tower is more than a neat feeling. That there's water worth fishing and fish worth catching in Minnesota's metropolis says something about the people who call themselves Twin Citians.

But can you hear the call of the loon in the metropolis?

Of course. Within the Twin Cities, there are a few loons that fly the lakes and there are a few other loons that walk the streets. If you fish the metro lakes long enough, you'll hear one or the other.

That's a promise.

Angling about town/

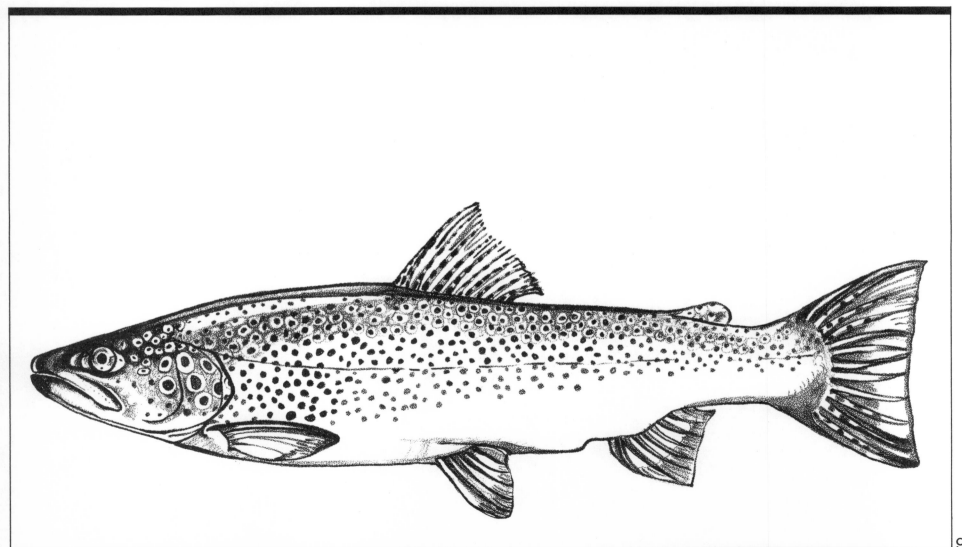

About do's and don'ts/

Fishing isn't always simple in the Twin Cities.

Nothing is simple when you have 200 lakes scattered in seven counties controlled by county commissioners, township officials, city councils, park boards and the state Department of Natural Resources.

These outfits like to make rules.

To fish in the Twin Cities lakes you need a valid Minnesota fishing license if you're between the ages of 16 and 64. If you're under 16 or if you're 65 or older, you don't need a fishing license. A resident license is $6.50.

Nonresidents 16 or older must have a nonresident Minnesota fishing license.

Fishing licenses are available at county courthouses and at sporting goods stores and bait shops. To fish trout, a $3 state trout stamp is required also.

So far, so good.

Keep in mind that the DNR establishes the fishing seasons and limits and requires a fishing license. However, local governments often control the lake accesses and each has its own set of rules.

On Lake Marion, the city-owned public access is free but a fee is charged for parking. Lakeville residents are allowed to park free along the street curbs but nonresidents are prohibited from doing same.

Huh?

On White Bear Lake, a city-owned access at Spiess Landing, formerly Matoska Park, allows residents to launch a boat and motor of any size. Nonresidents, however, are not allowed to launch a boat with a motor over 20 horsepower.

Huh?

On Square Lake, a county-owned public access cannot be used for boats of more than 10 horsepower. Next door at a private campground boats of any size outboard motor may be launched for a fee.

Huh?

The Minneapolis Park and Recreation Board operates differently. The board simply requires permits for just about everything connected with fishing, except standing on a fishing dock.

To operate an electric trolling motor, a $10 permit is required. To place a portable ice fishing shack on the Minneapolis city lakes,

a park board permit is required. Price of the permit is $12.50 for city residents; $18.50 for nonresidents.

The permits are available from the board's permit office on the 12th floor of the Summit Bank Bldg., 310 S. 4th St. in Minneapolis. The phone number is 348-5406.

Fishing is simpler in St. Paul's city lakes. No permit is required to use an electric trolling motor on Lake Phalen. Outboard motors are prohibited, however.

No permits are required to use the boat launches provided by the Ramsey County Parks and Recreation Dept.

Sometimes it doesn't pay to be an early morning angler in the Twin Cities. I ventured to Bryant Lake at dawn one morning and found a locked gate at the entrance to Bryant Lake Regional Park, the only boat access to the lake. A number of lake accesses in the Twin Cities are within county or city parks that "close" nightly and don't reopen until long past sunrise. Keep that in mind before you crawl out of bed with the chickens to do a little fishing.

A map of the Twin Cities region public lake accesses with information on special rules is available free by writing to: DNR-Metro Region, 1200 Warner Road, St. Paul 55106.

11

About wilderness lakes/

Wilderness is a word that's been kicked around lately. And in this discussion about wilderness fishing in the Twin Cities, my foot is swinging.

Once upon a time, wilderness was land ecologically unmolested by mankind. But it took an ecologist to identify true wilderness. Meanwhile, the rest of us knew only that ecology rhymed with biology and we flunked that in high school.

So most of us created our own definition of wilderness. Like the Twin City fisherman who called me one day and wanted to go fishing in the wilderness.

I dutifully advised the caller that he'd have to travel to the Far North or at least northeast Minnesota to find wilderness.

"No," he replied. "I want to fish in some wilderness around the Twin Cities."

Obviously the caller's definition of wilderness was a lake with trees instead of joggers on the shores.

No problem. There's plenty of wilderness fishing in the Twin Cities. Really. There are lakes surrounded by woodlands with nary a house or freeway in sight. Remarkably, these waters also are open to the public. So let's head for the . . . ah, wilderness:

Hyland Lake/
Tucked away within the Hyland Lake Park Reserve, Hyland Lake is a 100-acre hideaway loaded with largemouth bass and panfish. Fishing docks are available. Bring your own canoe or cartopper boat. Special fishing regulations prohibit the taking of bass between 12 to 16 inches. Bass under or over those lengths may be kept. The special bass rules are part of an experiment by the Department of Natural Resources to produce larger bluegills and a trophy bass fishery. The Hyland reserve, south of I-494 on East Bush Lake Road, is part of the Hennepin County Park Reserve District. A daily user fee of $2 is charged.

Bush Lake/
Adjacent to Hyland Lake, Bush Lake is part of wilderness-like Bloomington City Park on East Bush Lake Road. Public access is free. However, only fishing boats with a maximum of 6-horsepower outboards are permitted. High populations of northern pike and lunker bass lurk within this wilderness.

Lake Rebecca/
In Lake Rebecca Park Reserve, Rebecca is a tree-lined water of 252 acres harboring walleyes, largemouth bass and giant bullheads. Special fishing restrictions prohibit the taking of bass between 12 to 16 inches in length. Rental of rowboats and canoes is available. Electric trolling motors are permitted; outboards are prohibited. A boat launch is free. The Rebecca reserve, on County Road 50 south of Hwy. 55 near Rockford, is part of the Hennepin County Park Reserve District. A daily user fee of $2 is charged.

Lake Auburn/
A picturesque lake known for its northern pike and panfish, Auburn is within the Carver Park Reserve on Hwy. 5 east of Waconia. No boat or canoe rentals. The boat access to the 162-acre Auburn is free; there are no outboard restrictions.

Steiger (Victoria) Lake/
A rather plain-looking lake but still . . . ah, wilderness. Steiger also is within the Carver Park Reserve near the city limits of Victoria. The lake is known for its panfish and northern pike. There's a motor restriction of 10 horsepower; no rowboat or canoe rental. Public access is free.

About city trout/

Sure you can catch trout in the Twin Cities if you're smarter than the fish.

There are two trout lakes and one viable trout stream within the metro area that are stocked regularly with trout by the Department of Natural Resources.

Trout are not dumb, however. And these city trout are no different.

Trout are cautious fish with eagle eyes. All of which means you can't cast bass-sized plugs with 10-pound test line and really expect to fool a trout.

The best trout gear consists of ultra-light tackle with 2- to 4-pound test line. Or, the usual trout tackle, a fly rod outfit to cast artificial flies and tiny spinners.

If you're prepared to pursue these finicky fish, you don't have to go far.

Brown's Creek/
Brown's Creek empties into the St. Croix River just north of Stillwater. Stocked once a year by DNR fisheries crews, the stream harbors a moderate population of brown trout. Some lunkers in the range of 17 inches. Best fishing is in the lower 1¼ miles of Brown's Creek from the mouth to the Stone Bridge.

Square Lake/
In Washington County, Square Lake is one of the clearest lakes in the state and popular with scuba divers. Now managed as a trout lake, Square has been stocked by DNR with brown and rainbow trout. Good odds for a lunker brown of 8 pounds or more. A county-owned public access, on the east end, has a posted limit of 10 horsepower or less for boat launching. The 10-horse restriction does not apply to the lake, however. Boats and outboards of any size may be launched for a fee at Golden Acres Campground, adjacent to the county park.

Courthouse Lake/
A favorite with winter fishermen, Courthouse Lake in Chaska is regularly stocked with rainbow trout. Shore fishing is possible. A few lunkers possible. No boat or canoe rental.

Trout Live Baits: nightcrawlers, worms, salmon eggs, canned kernel corn, marshmallows, small minnows.

Trout Lures: small spinners, spoons, diving plugs, lead-head jigs of $\frac{1}{32}$- to $\frac{1}{64}$-ounce size, artificial flies (wet, dry, nymphs and streamers).

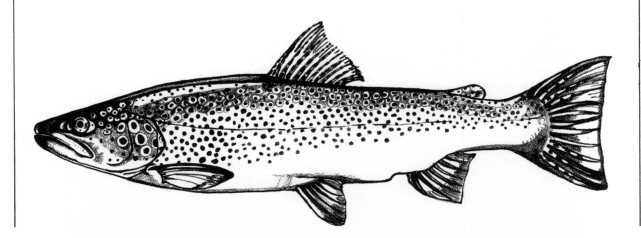

About ponds for kids/

The shore is where most fishermen begin and end.

They begin on shore as youngsters learning to fish. And they come back to shore as elderly anglers no longer able to handle the tasks of fishing from a boat.

In the Twin Cities area, neither the youngsters nor the oldsters have been forgotten.

There are some 21 ponds scattered about the metro region that are annually stocked by the Department of Natural Resources with catchable sunfish, crappies and bullheads. Sunfish will weigh up to half a pound and crappies up to three quarters.

Although known as "kids' ponds" the waters are open to anglers of all ages.

Most ponds are shallow and will not support fish life over winter. Other ponds may be affected by periods of drought. Consequently, the up-to-date list of stocked ponds may vary from summer to summer. For information on ponds and their stocking schedule, contact the DNR Metro Region offices, Fisheries Section, 1200 Warner Road, St. Paul 55106.

Ponds For Kids

Blaine
Loch Ness Park
Fridley
Moore Lake
Chaska
Chaska Swimming Pool Pond
Burnsville
Burnsville Pond
Eagan
Carlson Lake
West St. Paul
Marthaler Pond
Inver Grove Heights
Simley Pond
Edina
Birchcrest Pond
Maple Grove
Boundary Creek Pond
Champlin
Champlin Mill Pond
Brooklyn Center
Civic Center Pond
Minneapolis
Kasota Pond, north of Kasota Ave.
Webber Pond, northwest
   of Webber Parkway
Wirth Lake
Powderhorn Lake
Richfield
Taft Lake

Bloomington
Winchester Pond
Lower Penn Lake
Roseville
Bennett Lake
Shoreview
Judy Lake
St. Paul
Loeb Lake
Jordan
Jordan Mill Pond

Fishing ponds also are in William O'Brien State Park (Alice Lake) and on the Minnesota Valley Trail (Beason Lake).

About shore fishing/

A shore fisherman in the Twin Cities must first find a friendly shore.

There's plenty of fishing water. But there are also plenty of "no parking" signs, plenty of "no trespassing" signs and plenty of aquatic weeds to give a shore angler fits.

Fortunately there are also plenty of fish to be caught from shore in the Twin Cities. Despite the boat jams on Lake Minnetonka, upward of 40 percent of all the fishing on the lake takes place from land, according to surveys by the Department of Natural Resources.

Shore fishing is popular because it's a relatively safe, economical sport that doesn't require much more than patience to watch a bobber.

Most of the shore fishing opportunities in the Twin Cities are for panfish. Other sport fishes may be nabbed while you stand on the banks but consistent catches are rare.

Finding a place to fish from shore is the catch, to coin an unpardonable pun. Boaters demand launch sites and marinas but who stomps the governmental halls for the shore fisherman? Nobody. That's why some "public" lakes have become nearly isolated from the public. Lake Marion is one of the unfriendliest lakes in the Twin Cities. Roads along the lakeshore are littered with "no parking" signs, clearly aimed at keeping the shore fisherman away.

Still, there are places where shore anglers are welcomed. Public fishing docks have been built on several of the Minneapolis city lakes. Elsewhere, garbage cans and toilet facilities are often provided at popular shore-fishing sites.

How long these shore-fishing luxuries will be provided will depend on the shore angler. The surest way to get a "no fishing" sign is to leave the worm cans and candy wrappers on the shore instead of in the garbage cans.

Public fishing docks: Fishing docks are provided on seven Minneapolis lakes by the Minneapolis Parks and Recreation Board. The lakes are Nokomis, Calhoun, Cedar, Harriet, Wirth, Brownie and Hiawatha.

Other fishing docks are at Long Lake in New Brighton and Taft Lake in Richfield.

Although most lakes within the metro area are surrounded by private homes, shore fishing is available. A few private landowners will permit access by permission to shore anglers. Still other lakes are within public parks. The following lakes have shore-fishing areas open to the public.

Shore Fishing Sites/
Lake/Location
Lake Minnetonka/Wayzata
Hyland Lake/Hyland Park Reserve
Lake Rebecca/Rebecca Park Reserve
Mississippi River/Coon Rapids Dam, Minnehaha Creek, Ford Dam, various other sites.
Rum River/Anoka
Minnesota River/Shakopee
St. Croix River/Afton State Park
Lake Peltier/Centerville
White Bear Lake/White Bear
Keller Lake/Maplewood
Lake Phalen/St. Paul
Silver Lake/North St. Paul
Lake Vadnais/Vadnais Heights
Sucker Lake/Vadnais Heights
Snail Lake/Shoreview
Long Lake/New Brighton
Lake Josephine/Arden Hills
Lake Johanna/Arden Hills
Twin Lakes/Crystal
Crystal Lake/Robbinsdale
Lake Como/St. Paul
Bush Lake/Bloomington
Crystal Lake/Burnsville
Marion Lake/Lakeville
Cedar Lake/New Prague
O'Dowd Lake/Shakopee
Lake Ann/Chanhassen
Lake Steiger/Carver Park Reserve
Lake Auburn/Carver Park Reserve

15

Eagle Lake/Young America
Lake Zumbra/Carver Park Reserve
Lake Independence/Baker Park Reserve
Lake George/Anoka
Lake Bavaria/Victoria
Waconia Lake/Waconia
Bald Eagle/White Bear Lake
Bass Lake/Plymouth

About metro minnows/

Code: m-minnows; n-nightcrawlers; w-worms; l-leeches; ww-waxworms

Belle Plaine/
Dave's Bait
100 East Main
Belle Plaine 56011
1-873-6144 (home) 1-873-9203 (bar)
Monday-Saturday 8:30 a.m. to 10 p.m.
m,n,w,l,ww

Coon Rapids/
Haven's Sporting Goods
2141 Coon Rapids Blvd.
Coon Rapids 55433
755-5040
Monday and Tuesday 9 a.m. to 7 p.m.;
Wednesday, Thursday and Friday 9 a.m. to
9 p.m.; Saturday 6 a.m. to 5 p.m.; Sunday
6 a.m. to noon
m,n,w,l,ww

Elk River/
Ebner's Live Bait
17015 Hwy. 10 NW.
Elk River 55330
441-1550
24 hours a day
m,n,w,l,ww

Excelsior/
Roy's Live Bait
360 Hwy. 7
Excelsior 55331
474-0927
5 a.m. to 8 p.m. 7 days a week
m,n,w,l,ww, frogs

Leach's Resort
7001 Minnewashta Pkwy.
Excelsior 55331
474-8135
7 a.m. to 8 p.m. 7 days a week (5/15-9/15)
m,n,w,ww

Forest Lake/
Tim's Sporting Good Store
67 S. Lake St.
Forest Lake 55025
464-3804
Monday-Friday 6 a.m. to 8 p.m.; Saturday
6 a.m.-6 p.m.; Sunday 6 a.m.-5 p.m.
m,n,w,l,ww

Timm's Marina
9080 Jewell Lane
Forest Lake 55025
464-9965 or 464-3890
May-Oct. 5:30 a.m.-11 p.m.
m,n,w,l

Hastings/
Hastings Farm Market and Garden Center
1419 Vermillion St.
Hastings 55035
437-8544
8 a.m.-8 p.m. 7 days a week (April to Oct.)
(Oct. to April 8 a.m. to 6 p.m.)
m,n,w,l,ww

Hub's Bait House
Hastings 55035
437-4358
6 a.m.-6 p.m. 7 days a week
m,n,w,l,ww

Lake Elmo/
Pierre's Pier
Cty. Rd. 17
Lake Elmo
770-0094 or 777-1642
4 a.m.-9 p.m. weekends; 7 a.m.-9 p.m.
weekdays (May 1 to Oct. 1)
m,n,l,w

Lakeville/
Frank's Bait Shop
17576 Kenwood Trail West
Lakeville 55044
435-5528
Monday-Friday 6 a.m. to 10 p.m.; Saturday
and Sunday 5 a.m. to 10 p.m. (Winter 7
a.m. to 10 p.m., 7 days a week)
m,n,w,l,ww

Marine-St. Croix /
Shady Birch Resort
17543 Lisbon Av. N.
Marine-St. Croix 55047
433-3391
Monday-Friday 8 a.m. to 8 p.m.; Saturday
and Sunday 5 a.m. to 9 p.m. m,n,w,l,

Mound /
Bob's Bait Shop
2630 Commerce Blvd.
Mound 55364
472-1884
Monday-Thursday, 6 a.m. to 7 p.m.; Friday,
6 a.m. to 8 p.m.; Saturday 5 a.m. to 8
p.m.; Sunday 5 a.m. to 7 p.m. (Open 1
hour later after Labor Day)
m,n,w,l,ww

Martin's and Sons
4858 Edgewater Dr.
Mound 55364
472-1220
dawn to dusk, 7 days a week; closed winter m,n,w

New Hope /
Archie's Standard Bait and Tackle
9400 36th Av. N.
New Hope 55427
545-6886
6 a.m. to 10 p.m. days a week
m,n,w,l,ww

Oakdale /
Blue Ribbon Bait and Taxidermy
1985 Geneva Av.
Oakdale 55119
777-2421
6 a.m. to 8 p.m. 7 days a week
m,n,w,l,ww

Orono
Paul's Landing
County Rd. 15; Smith's Bay
Orono 55323
473-0281
dawn to dusk, 7 days a week
m,n,w,l,ww

Osseo /
Lenarz Resort
6153 Eagle Lake Dr.
Osseo 55369
535-1393
6 a.m. to 10 p.m. 7 days a week
m,n,w,l,ww

Plymouth /
Markham Sports Unlimited
18110 Hwy. 55
Plymouth 55446
478-6721
Monday-Friday 6 a.m. to 8 p.m.; Saturday
6 a.m. to 6 p.m.; Sunday 6 a.m. to 5 p.m.
(winter open at 7:30 a.m.)
m,n,w,l,ww

Harty's Boat and Bait
1920 E. Medicine Lake Blvd.
Plymouth 55446
546-3849
Hours vary according to time of year
m,n,w,ww

Prior Lake /
J & D Sporting Goods
15760 Hwy. 13
Prior Lake 55372
447-6096
Monday-Friday 6 a.m. to 8 p.m.; Saturday
and Sunday 5 a.m. to 7 p.m.
m,n,w,l,ww

Hadac's Bait Shop
16154 Main Av. SE.
Prior Lake 55372
447-2632
6 a.m. to 8 p.m. 7 days a week
m,n,w,l,ww

Richfield /
Al's Bait and Shoe Service
1308 E. 66th St.
Richfield 55423
866-5640
Closed Monday; Tuesday-Friday 7 a.m. to
7:30 p.m.; Saturday 6 a.m. to 6 p.m.; Sunday 6 a.m. to 4 p.m.
m,n,w,l,ww

Shorewood/
Howard Point Marina
5400 Howard Point Road
Shorewood 55331
474-4464
Sunup to sundown, summer hours; 8 a.m.
to 5 p.m. winter hours
m,n,w,ww

Spring Lake Park/
John Vados Bait Company
7895 Hwy. 65
Spring Lake Park 55432
784-6728
Monday-Friday 6 a.m. to 8 p.m.; Saturday
and Sunday 5 a.m to 8 p.m.
m,n,w,l,ww, frogs

Spring Park/
Don's Bait
4120 Spring St.
Spring Park 55384
471-9311
6 a.m. to 6 p.m. 7 days a week (April/
May/June 5 a.m. to 8 p.m.)
m,n,w,l,ww

Shoreline Bait and Tackle
4030 Shoreline Dr.
Spring Park 55384
471-7876
5 a.m. to 9 p.m. 7 days a week
m,n,w,l,ww

St. Michael/
Dale's 66 (Phillips)
101 Central Av.
St. Michael 55376
497-2666
Monday-Friday 5:30 a.m. to 8 p.m.; Saturday 7 a.m. to 8 p.m.; Sunday 8 a.m. to 4
p.m.
m,n,w,l,ww

St. Paul/
Gimp's Bait and Sporting Goods
1239 Rice St.
St. Paul 55117
489-7988
7 a.m. to 8 p.m. 7 days a week
m,n,w,l,ww

Harvey's Bait Store
2616 Rice St.
St. Paul 55113
484-7923
6 a.m. to 9 p.m. 7 days a week
m,n,w,l,ww

Northland Bait
235 East Wyoming
St. Paul 55107
291-0995
6 a.m. to 11 p.m. 7 days a week
m,n,w,ww

Waconia/
In Towne Marina
8 East Lake St.
Waconia 55387
442-2096
6:30 a.m. to 9 p.m. summer; 7 a.m. to 7
p.m. winter
m,n,w,l,ww

Waconia Marina
308 E. Lake St.
Waconia 55387
448-6122
5 a.m. to 10 p.m. 7 days a week
m,n,w,l,ww, frogs

Wayzata
Gray's Bay Marina
2831 Hwy. 101 S.
Wayzata 55391
473-2550
dawn to dark, 7 days a week' 7 a.m. to 6
p.m.
m,n,w,l,ww

Fishing the cities/

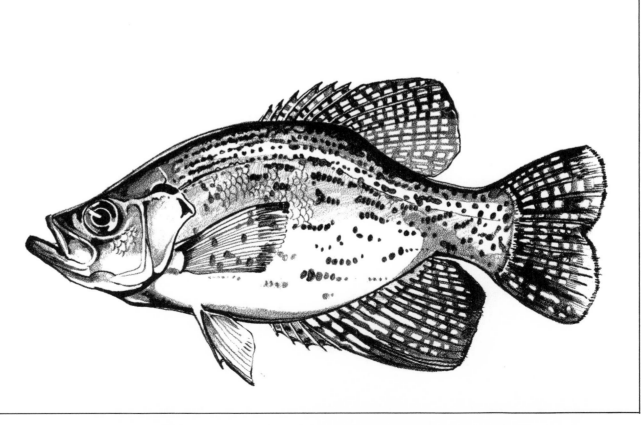

City panfish/

Believe it or not, there are in the Twin Cities more panfish than orange road-construction barricades.

There are panfish in every lake in the metro region, not to mention ditches, aquariums and storm sewers. There are so many panfish that the Department of Natural Resources estimates that sunfish, bluegills and crappies account for more than half of all fish caught in the Twin Cities.

Unfortunately, many fishermen make catching panfish more difficult. They use fishing line heavier than baling twine and a bobber larger than a volleyball. It just isn't necessary. Most bluegills and crappies in Twin Cities waters won't weigh a pound, which means a light monofilament line of about 4-pound test is sufficient. And you'll catch more fish.

If you can't see a small bobber, get eyeglasses.

Panfish are relatively easy to catch but they don't jump into the boat or onto the stringer. Use of the proper tackle, however, will almost ensure success. Unlike other gamefish, panfish always seem to be in a biting mood. If you're doing a few things right.

(Bluegills and sunfish really are two different species. However, they are treated as one

and, indeed, the two species often are difficult to distinguish.)

Panfish gear /

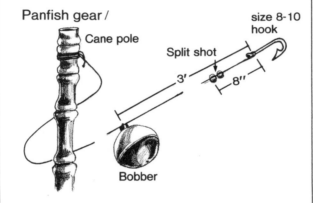

Cane pole

Split shot

size 8-10 hook

3'

8''

Bobber

Panfish gear for kids: Keep the fishing tackle simple. For youngsters under the age of 10, a cane pole is ideal. Cane poles are available at sporting goods stores and sell for under $5. Add line, bobber, splitshot and a hook.

Panfish gear for older kids: For kids of any age over 10, the best panfishing gear consists of a light-action fishing rod and a spin-cast reel (push-button type). Spool the reel with 4- to 6-pound test line.

(Unlike cane poles, the spin-cast outfit can be used for casting, a definite advantage. A child under 10 could handle such a task but

it's like inviting trouble. Sooner or later trouble will arrive in the form of a hook in the bushes or seat of the pants.)

What goes on the business end of the fishing line may vary. A small hook, splitshot and bobber for live bait are surely adequate.

A specially-designed bobber, called a "slip-bobber," may be more practical. The slip-bobber makes it easy to fish at greater depths and still cast, since the bobber slips up the line for casting. After the cast, the line slips back through the bobber until it stops at a prescribed depth. Slip bobbers are available at tackle stores.

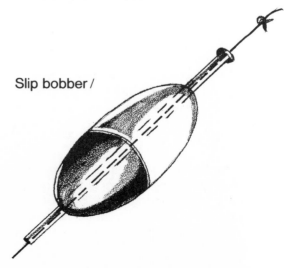

Slip bobber /

Catching city sunfish/bluegills/

The odds are in your favor. On almost every lake bank in the Twin Cities region, there's a sunfish or bluegill within casting distance. Every dock, every bridge, every patch of aquatic weeds will have panfish nearby.

The problem is (if you can call catching fish a problem) the bulk of the sunnies and bluegills will be small, maybe quarter-pounders. So what? It'll take longer to clean the fish but the taste is the same.

Larger bluegills (one-half pound or bigger) do exist, however. The best time to find the heftier bluegills is in late May or early June when the fish move into the shallows to spawn.

For the rest of the summer, the larger bluegills hang in deeper water on the outside edge of weedbeds. In the metropolitan lakes, the ''weedline'' (the depth at which weeds stop growing) ranges from 4 to more than 20 feet. Clear lakes will have a deeper weedline; in murky waters the weedline may be nonexistent.

Without the aid of a boat it's almost impossible to fish the deeper waters outside a weedbed. If you're shorebound, look for other features on a lake that attract bluegills, such as shady waters under docks and bridges, fallen treetops or brush.

Where bluegills hang out in the summer/

Fortunately bluegills and sunfish open their mouths rather willingly. But their mouths don't open very wide. This evolutionary fact requires that small baits and lures be offered. Tiny jigs of $\frac{1}{32}$- to $\frac{1}{64}$-ounce sizes are ideal. Artificial wet flies, such as spiders made of sponge, also are excellent. Color choices may vary.

An ideal rig is to use a bobber and fly. Cast out and then slowly retrieve the fly. When the bobber jerks, a bluegill has taken the bait.

Another method is to fish without the bobber, using a small splitshot placed 12 to 18 inches above the artificial fly. Cast the splitshot and fly, allow it to sink momentarily and then slowly retrieve the lure. You'll feel the strike.

From a boat, cast the splitshot and fly, and then drift along the outside edge of the weedlines until you've made contact with a school of bluegills.

Bluegill/sunfish baits: Panfish eat anything. Live baits include earthworms (not nightcrawlers), crickets, wax worms.

25

Catching city crappies/

Crappies are to bluegills what oranges are to apples. Related but different. Like bluegills, crappies are found in waters throughout the metro area and the same fishing tackle may be used.

But it's the differences that count. Crappies love minnows whereas bluegills love bugs.

The simplest crappie-catching rig is a slip-bobber, a small splitshot and a long shank Aberdeen hook. Add a live minnow, no larger than 1½-inches, and you've got the original crappie killer.

Yet many successful crappie fishermen prefer to go with a small $\frac{1}{16}$- or $\frac{1}{32}$-ounce jig adorned with a minnow. The jig acts as an attracter, particularly if white, yellow or pink. Use a small bobber to float the jig at the desired depth. What's the desired depth? It's found by trial and error.

In Twin City lakes, the crappies move into shallow bays and linger for several weeks immediately after the ice goes off the lakes. It's the highlight of a crappie fisherman's year. The fish are easy to find and easy to catch. For what other reason do some 10,000 anglers annually flock to Lake Minnetonka for the Johnson-Holiday crappie contest held in late April?

In the spring, crappies may be caught at

Crappie rig/

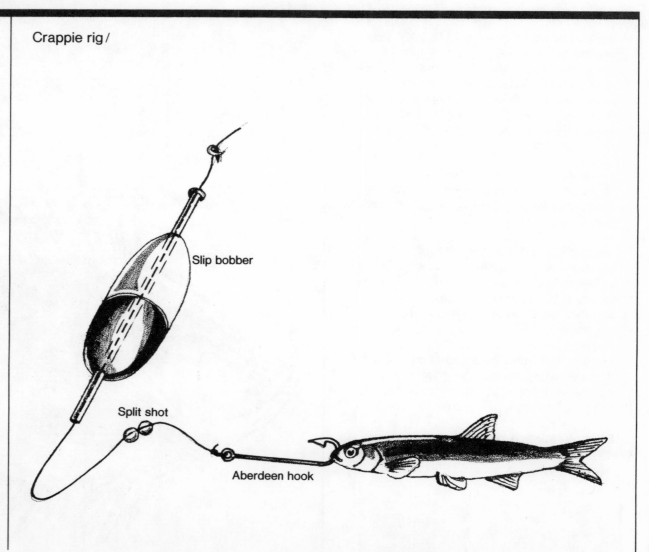

Slip bobber

Split shot

Aberdeen hook

depths of four feet or less. Later, however, the crappie schools tend to move off into deeper water of 10 to 20 feet or more. Still, crappies will linger near something, such as weedlines, sunken islands and the like. But there is no easy way of finding the schools, except by trial and error.

When you're searching, it helps to use live minnows for bait rather than a plain jig. Once you've located a school of crappies, then by all means test your skill by fishing without the use of live bait.

How do you fish a jig? The key is to use light-weight monofilament of no more than six-pound test. The light line allows for longer casts and more life-like action by the jig. How do you give "life" to a jig? By "jigging" it. Cast it out and pump it back. Try to imitate the darting swimming action of a minnow. And have confidence. For crappies or anything that swims, confidence is the key to catching.

Crappie baits: Crappies prefer small minnows (1 to 1½ inches long). Fish the minnow with a conventional hook or add the minnow to a small jig.

Best panfish waters: Lake Minnetonka, Big Carnelian, Lake Phalen, Calhoun, Medicine, Weaver, Big Marine, Forest, Waconia, Pierson, Square, Elmo, Minnewashta

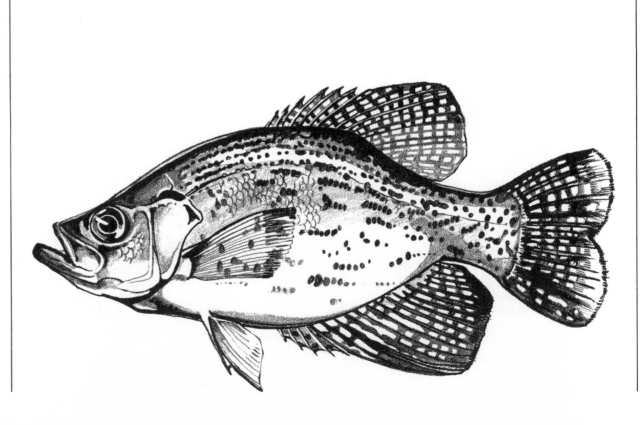

City walleyes/

Most Twin Cities fishermen really don't need to be told how to catch walleyes. Would you tell Californians how to drive on freeways?

Minnesota has more natural walleye water than any other state—which explains why half the resident anglers think they're walleye experts while the other half know for sure.

But catching the urban walleye is an angling frontier of its own. For one thing, few city anglers are aware that there are walleyes living south of Mille Lacs.

Lordy, there are walleyes in downtown Minneapolis and St. Paul via the Mississippi River. As nature intended, there are walleyes in the St. Croix River. And in the Minnesota River. And in the Rum River.

Keep an eye also on the Minnesota Department of Natural Resources stocking trucks. In recent years the DNR trucks have dumped millions of walleyes in Lake Harriet, of all places. Lake Minnetonka and White Bear Lake also have received huge doses of stocked walleyes.

And under the noses of all the walleye experts, these walleyes have grown to, well, as big as "up north." Would you believe there's an 11-pound walleye in Lake Harri-

Live bait rig/

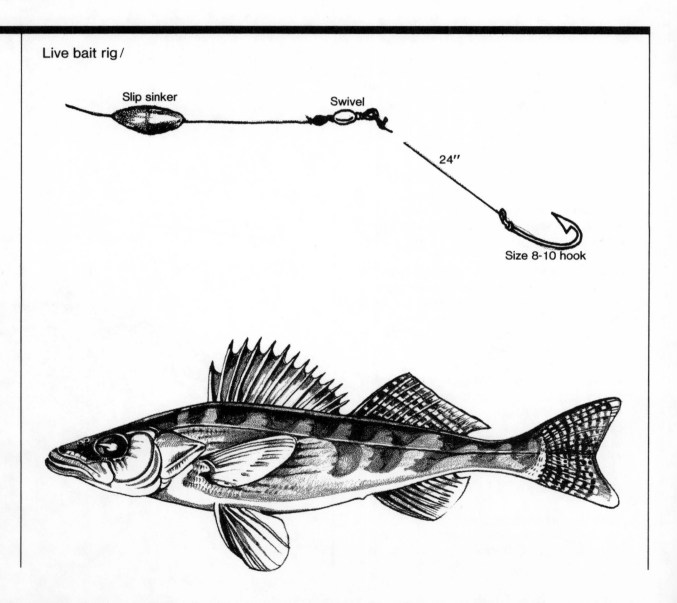

Slip sinker

Swivel

24"

Size 8-10 hook

et? Swimming in a circle, no doubt. The 11-pounder showed up in a DNR test net a couple of years ago. The lunker was released alive and hasn't been caught yet. Honest.

Goes to show you catching walleyes in the big cities is a new ball game.

Walleye tackle: A medium-action spinning outfit with 8- to 10-pound test monofilament is best. Spin-cast or casting reels also are adequate.

Walleye baits: The best walleye lures include: 1/8- to 3/8-ounce lead-head jigs, Lindy rigs and an assortment of live bait, such as nightcrawlers, minnows and leeches.

Catching city walleyes: City lakes often lack what the walleye naturally seeks. Lake Harriet, for example, is a bowl-shaped lake with scattered weedbeds. Not exactly typical walleye water.

But what can the walleye do? Move out? No, it must make do with what's available. Same goes for the other ''unnatural'' walleye waters in the metro region.

What it means is that the fisherman of city walleyes must be prepared to change fishing tactics when necessary.

Hooking live bait for walleye/

The walleye is a different character in many of the city lakes. It becomes a fish of the weedbeds, not unlike a northern pike. The aquatic vegetation, such as pondweed or "cabbage," provides the cover and shade the walleye needs. The weeds, of course, attract minnows and other walleye prey.

The problem is catching walleyes in weeds. Needless to say, it's difficult casting or trolling a minnow through a weedbed without getting snagged. At best, you only can cast or troll the weedbed edges.

Bobber fishing with a leech is an alternative, dropping the bait into pockets or along the weedline.

What's best? Take a lesson from the bass fishermen on Lake Minnetonka who throw the "weedless" plastic worms. The bass anglers have been catching walleyes. Why? Because they're angling the weedbeds where the bass AND walleyes roam. A walleye on the prowl has no qualms about inhaling a worm meant for a bass.

Frankly, don't expect to pile walleyes on the stringer under weedy conditions. The walleyes tend to be scattered and difficult to locate in the weedbeds. You'll likely catch one here, another there.

Rock reefs and gravel bars—the conventional walleye haunts—do exist on a few city lakes, such as White Bear Lake, Waconia and Minnetonka. And there are walleyes inhabiting those places.

A fishing friend, Dick Sternberg, nailed some 30 walleyes in Brown's Bay on Minnetonka one summer. Sternberg used the conventional walleye-catching method, drifting and trolling a Lindy rig with a leech on the edge of a reef in 22 feet of water.

River rig /

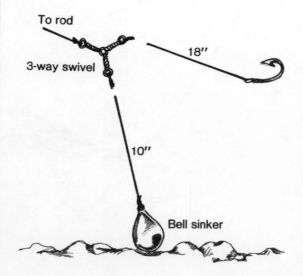

To rod

3-way swivel

18"

10"

Bell sinker

Walleyes in city rivers: The metro rivers, particularly the Mississippi and St. Croix, can produce excellent walleye fishing. The best river fishing technique is to drift over walleye haunts with a Lindy rig or a "river rig."

A river rig consists of a three-way swivel with a short line to a lead weight, a short line to the bait and a line to the rod.

As the name indicates, the river rig is best suited for fishing in a current.

Jig-minnow combinations also are popular among river anglers. In most cases, a jig of at least three-eighths ounce is necessary to reach bottom in the current. Most anglers merely drag the jig-minnow on the bottom or bounce it slightly until a walleye strikes. Rocks sometimes strike, of course, so be prepared to lose a few lures.

Best metro walleye waters /

Lakes: Minnetonka, White Bear, Harriet, Cedar (Scott County), Waconia, Forest, Phalen, Rebecca, Prior.

Rivers: Mississippi, Minnesota, St. Croix.

City largemouth bass/

Next time somebody asks why you live in the Twin Cities, say you're a bassin' boy. Say you're obsessed with chasing hawg jaws.

It could be the truth.

Fact is, the waters of the Twin Cities harbor some of the best largemouth bass fishing in Minnesota.

Call it piscatorial justice.

City lakes tend to be overlooked by most of the angling fraternity. Many fishermen simply cannot understand how a bass can do its thing in a crowd.

But the bass does. I've had bass suck up a plastic worm in Lake of the Isles while afternoon canoeists paddled over my fishing line.

Most of the Twin City lakes are natural bass waters, featuring soft bottoms, lily pads, cabbage weeds and plenty of food. Under these ideal conditions, the bass in the Twin Cities have become relatively abundant—and greatly ignored.

No wonder the city lakes annually yield big-bellied hawg jaws, those 6- to 8-pounders.

To a bassin' boy, that's reason enough to become a city slicker.

Bass gear: A medium- to heavy-action rod with a spinning reel or spincast reel. Optional gear is a casting rod with a baitcast reel. Line test of 8 to 12 pounds.

Bass live bait: frog, minnow, leech, crayfish, nightcrawler.

Bass lures: plastic worm, spinnerbait, crankbait, topwater, lead-head jig.

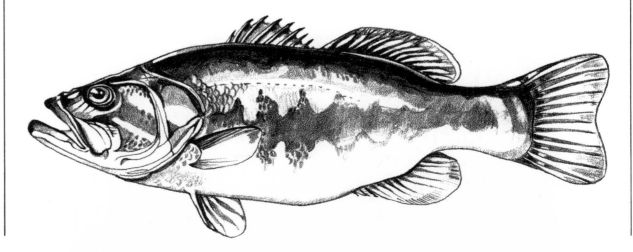

Catching city bass/

Largemouth bass in the Twin Cities are almost always found in one of two places on a lake: In the shallow, weedy bays or at the edge of deep-water weedlines.

Where and how you pursue bass depends on the lake and the bass habitat therein. In lakes such as Minnetonka or Waconia, both types of bass cover are available, and bass roam in both areas. In lakes such as Independence and Bald Eagle, only shallow, weedy bays are present. The deep-water weedlines are absent because of murky waters.

Still other lakes, such as Calhoun and Lake

George, are without shallow, weedy bays. Consequently, most of the bass will be found in or on the outside edge of deeper, submerged weedbeds.

Fishing the shallow, weedy bays requires the use of weedless lures, such as spinner-baits, Johnson spoons, topwater lures and plastic worms. Best hours are early morning and late evenings. But don't pass up shallow-water bass fishing simply because you overslept. A largemouth bass has no qualms about smashing a surface lure amid the lily pads at high noon.

Also, don't underestimate the depth of wa-

ter where bass may be found. So it's August and the air is hot and humid and you're sweating like a butcher hog. So you think all the bass in the lake are cooling off in some deep water haunt. Don't be foolish. On the hottest days a bass can be quite content in two feet of water under the shade of a lily pad patch.

Bass lurking in deeper water along the weedlines are more difficult to find. On the other hand, weedline bass are catchable by the angler who can't get out of bed before 9 in the morning.

It's important to understand that the depth

Largemouth bass hangouts/

Deep weedline drop-off

Shallow weed flats

of weedlines varies considerably in Twin Cities lakes, depending on the clarity of the water. The clearer the water, the deeper the sunlight penetrates. Submerged aquatic vegetation requires sunlight.

One method of fishing the weedline is with a plastic worm. Fish the plastic worm in one of two ways known as the Texas Rig or Bollig's Rig. Simply cast the worm toward the weedbeds, allow the worm to sink, then slowly work the worm toward the outside of the weedbed. When the bass inhales the imitation, you'll feel a ''thunk.'' That's all. Just a thunk. Set the hook.

Sometimes bass on a weedline are looking up, however. When that happens, the best two lures are the diving crankbaits and sinking spinnerbaits. Merely cast and retrieve both lures over and alongside the weedlines. The bass will take care of the rest.

It is also possible to troll alongside the weedlines with deep-diving lures.

Lakes such as Minnetonka may have miles of weedlines. So where do you start? Look for weedline points or inside turns of a weedline. These two places usually hold the bass.

And don't forget to practice some fish conservation with bass. The fish is more excit-

ing to catch than to fry in a pan. For that reason, more and more bassin' boys are releasing the bass alive to catch them again another day.

Best bass lakes: Minnetonka, George, Weaver, Waconia, Zumbra, Calhoun, Cedar, Johanna, Big Carnelian, Elmo, Jane, White Bear, Prior.

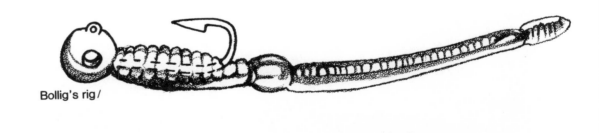

Bollig's rig/

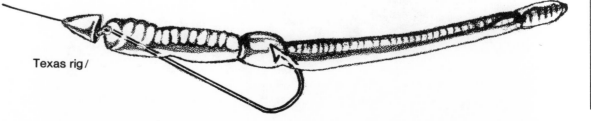

Texas rig/

City muskies/northern pike/

Northern pike and the mighty muskellunge are fish of the wilderness where loons call and water laps in country untouched and unmarred by man.

Welcome to the wilderness of the Twin Cities.

In St. Paul and Minneapolis, northern pike swim in waters turned green by lawn fertilizer and muskies roam in lakes surrounded by joggers and bikers.

And you know what? The pike and muskies are doing fine, thank you.

Pike and muskies are closely related cousins, fish with almost matching bodies connected to a pair of toothy jaws.

Both fish species live in similar haunts—that is, muskies and pike are fish of the weedbeds in the city wilderness. To the untrained eye, muskies and northern pike may appear to look alike. There are differences, however. Remember: a northern pike is dark with light spots; a muskie is light with dark spots. Proper identification is important because it is illegal to keep a muskie that is under 30 inches in length. There are no size restrictions on northern pike.

Muskie/

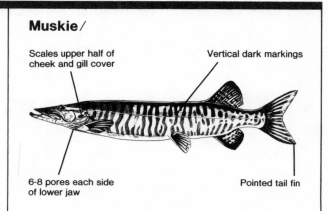

Scales upper half of cheek and gill cover

Vertical dark markings

6-8 pores each side of lower jaw

Pointed tail fin

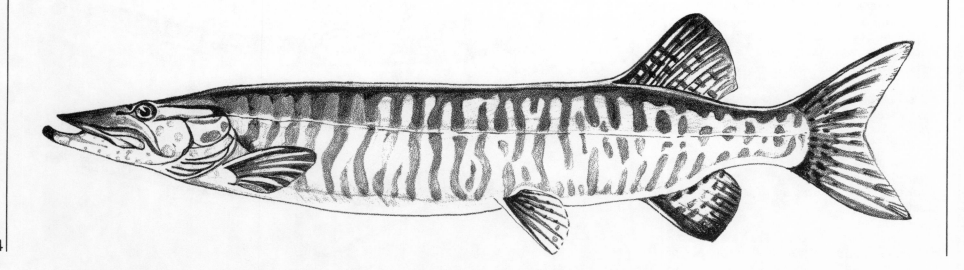

34

Almost all waters in the metropolitan region harbor northern pike. It is a popular fish among city anglers, second only to panfish.

Northern pike gear: Medium- to heavy-action rod with spinning, spin-cast or bait-casting reel. Line test of 10 to 17 pounds. A 6- to 12-inch steel leader is a must.

Muskie gear: Heavy-action rod with bait-casting reel. Line test of 17 to 30 pounds. A 12-inch steel leader is a must.

Pike live bait: Large 4-inch sucker minnow, nightcrawler.

Muskie live bait: Large 6-inch sucker minnow.

Pike lures: Spoons, diving plugs, jig-minnow, spinnerbaits, spinners, plastic worm.

Muskie lures: Bucktail spinners, jerk baits, diving plugs, jig-minnow, plastic worm, topwater.

Northern pike/

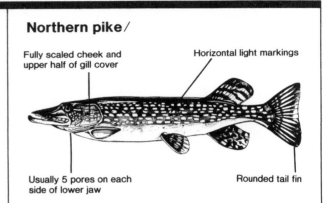

Fully scaled cheek and upper half of gill cover

Horizontal light markings

Usually 5 pores on each side of lower jaw

Rounded tail fin

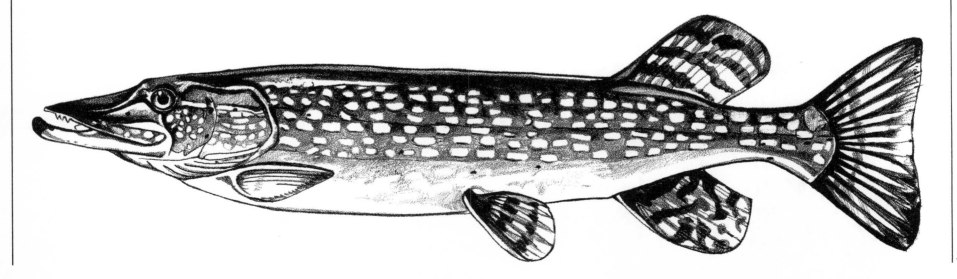

Catching city pike/

Troll, drift or cast. All three methods will take northern pike if the lure is placed in the right areas.

And what are the right areas? Back to the weedline, that spot in a lake where the aquatic vegetation ceases to grow. Pike hang in and around these weedbeds, preferably those with deepwater drops nearby.

Also look for pike on lakes where rock reefs or sunken islands exist, such as on Lake Minnetonka, Waconia or White Bear. Aquatic weeds may or may not be present on these sunken islands and reefs. But if food, such as perch, is present the northern pike won't be far away.

Like the bass, pike don't always need deep water. On Lake Independence, for example, the pike will be found in water less than 5 feet deep because the weedline is no deeper.

Trolling and casting are popular pike catching methods on the city lakes. But one of my favorite techniques is to drift the edge of a weedline with a ¼-ounce jig tipped with a small sucker minnow.

Speed trolling also is effective. Lake Minnetonka guide George Kuffel prefers to troll fast with a deep-diving Bomber plug. He regularly nails nice pike when other methods fail.

Best northern pike waters: Eagle, Medicine, Minnetonka, Cedar, Bush, Forest Lake, Waconia, Weaver.

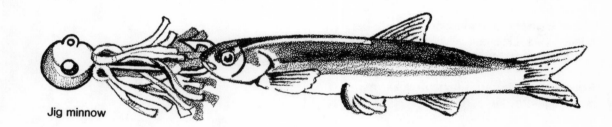

Jig minnow

Catching city muskies/

No fish is more cherished in all fresh water than the muskie. Yet it's possible for the city angler to fulfill that dream catch within sight of downtown Minneapolis.

It's work. Casting is the usual means of chasing muskies. And, as they say, it takes 10,000 casts to catch a muskie. However, trolling also works, although it is less exciting. The fisherman who casts often sees a muskie follow the lure. A muskie follow is one of the most exciting moments in sport fishing.

Regardless of the method, muskies share the same hangouts in a lake with northern pike. Again, these hangouts are on the edge of the weedbeds and in the weedy bays.

The most potent weapon available to a muskie fisherman is the bucktail spinner. Best colors are black, yellow, white and red. The bucktail can be cast or trolled. It can be fished deep or shallow.

Keep in mind that the muskies in the Twin Cities waters tend to be shallow-water fish during the summer. An exception might be Minnetonka, where deep-water weedbeds are present.

The notorious muskellunge is not quite as abundant or as popular. But the fact that muskies are available to anglers in the Twin Cities is material for Ripley's ''Believe It or Not.''

Legal-sized muskies now swim in Lake Harriet, Lake Minnetonka, Lake Independence and the St. Croix River. A long shot at muskies would be the Twin Cities stretch of the Mississippi River.

The city muskies originally were stocked more than a decade ago by the Department of Natural Resources. Today there are muskies of more than 20 pounds swimming in the city.

Which proves only one thing. A muskie is no easy catch. In the wilderness with trees. Or the wilderness with streets.

Best muskie waters: Independence, Harriet, Minnetonka.

City smallmouth bass/

Most Twin City residents believe the Mississippi River is severely polluted as it flows through the metropolis.

But nobody has asked the smallmouth bass.

If the smallmouth could talk, it might ask for bluer water but the fish wouldn't complain about toilet bowls. Fact is, the bronze-sided fish is an indicator of water quality. Smallmouth can't survive if the water is bad.

So there they are, smallmouth bass swimming and finning in the old Mississip as she rambles through the metropolis. This is the same feisty smallmouth that entertains the canoe fisherman in the Boundary Waters Canoe Area Wilderness.

So if you are a city-bound fisherman with a yen to tangle with a smallmouth, don't apologize to anybody.

What's more, there's plenty of smallmouth to tangle with. High populations of "smallies" abound in the Mississippi, Rum and St. Croix Rivers, those portions that flow by the metropolitan area. Smallmouth also swim in the waters of Lake Minnetonka and White Bear.

Smallmouth gear: Light- to medium-action rod with spin-cast or spinning reel. Line test of 4 to 6 pounds.

Smallmouth live bait: crayfish, leeches, minnows, nightcrawlers, frogs.

Smallmouth lures: spinners, diving plugs, jig-minnow, jig-spinners, streamer flies.

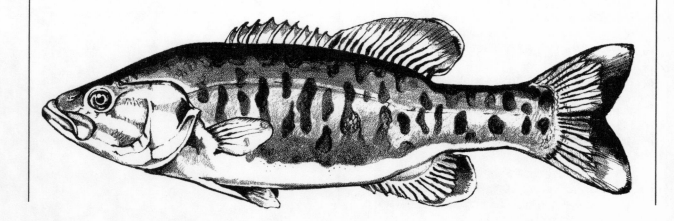

Catching city smallmouth/

Remember: smallmouth means small lures.

Smallmouth bass definitely prefer to eat daintily, not heartily, compared with their largemouth cousins. Ignore that rule and you'll get skunked over the best of smallmouth waters in the Twin Cities.

Remember also that smallmouth are to rocks what leaves are to trees. They're never very far apart. That's why most of the smallies in Lake Minnetonka are found in the rocky Smith and Brown's Bays and seldom elsewhere. That's also why the rocky rapids and shores, and not the muddy banks, are the best smallmouth haunts on the rivers.

Because the smallies are so rock-oriented, the fish are often easier to locate. I remember floating the St. Croix and catching smallmouth by skipping the mud banks and casting only to the rocky shorelines.

Locating smallmouth is only part of the puzzle, however. Which brings us back to the small-lure rule. Most spinners are available in various blade sizes, starting at No. 0, the smallest. For smallies, I'd suggest never using spinners larger than No. 2. Spinners with plain hooks or squirrel tails are excellent, such as the Mepps or Vibrax.

Another smallmouth fooler is a small, ⅛-

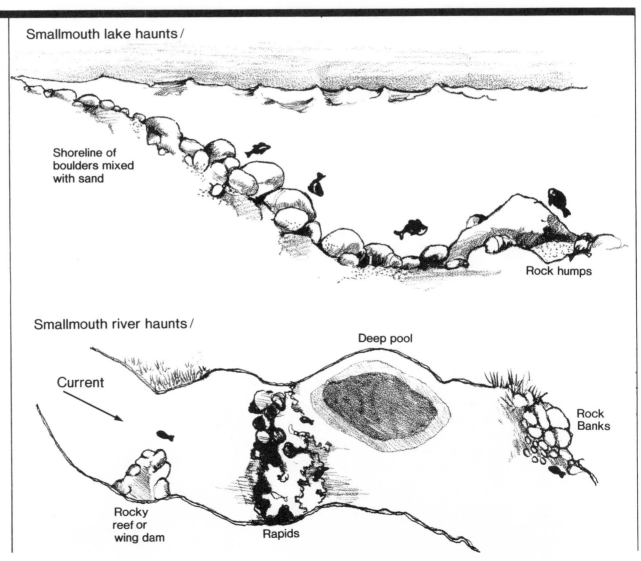

Smallmouth lake haunts/

Shoreline of boulders mixed with sand

Rock humps

Smallmouth river haunts/

Deep pool

Current

Rock Banks

Rocky reef or wing dam

Rapids

ounce jig and spinner combination, such as the Ugly Bug Plus or Beetle Spin.

Diving plugs, such as the smallest Rapala on the market, also are proven smallie getters.

Lake fishing for smallmouth can be more difficult as the fish tends to hang in deep 15 to 20 feet of water during midsummer.

Live bait is often more productive in deep water conditions, particularly on Minnetonka and White Bear Lake.

It's best to present the live bait in a simple fashion, using a splitshot or slip sinker and a plain hook. Cast or troll the bait over the deep-water haunts.

If you enjoy using artificial lures, there's another compromise. Try a ⅛-ounce jig adorned with a minnow, leech, pork rind or half of a nightcrawler.

If you have problems going small, it's probably because of the size of your fishing line. When casting light tackle it's important to use light line no heavier than six-pound test. Heavier line, say 10-pound test, will reduce your casting distance and your action.

And that's almost sinful. The smallmouth bass has a fighting heart as big as any in freshwater. The golden fish deserves to be

released to fight again another day.

Best smallmouth waters: St. Croix River, Rum River, Lake Minnetonka, White Bear Lake.

Jig spinner combination/

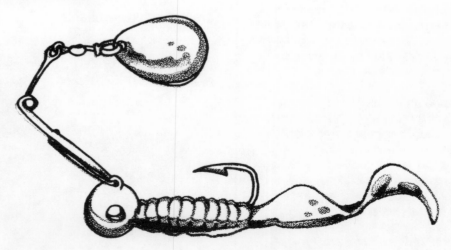

City catfish/bullheads/

Let's put it this way: To fish catfish and bullheads, you've got to love them.

Few fish are uglier than this bewhiskered duo.

Yet bullhead fishing is popular among Twin Cities anglers and the catfish has its own circle of diehard fans.

There are reasons. Ain't no fish easier to catch than a bullhead. It'll eat anything on a hook. Which is why bullheads never get any respect. Except in the frying pan. There aren't many fish that can beat a bullhead in the pan.

Beyond that, the bullhead's popularity is a mystery. As a fighting fish on the hook, the bullhead ranks just above a wet T-shirt. With sharp spines in its dorsal and pectoral fins, the bullhead is difficult to handle and even more difficult to fillet.

The channel catfish has got a little more class. It'll smack an artificial lure and make a fishing reel squeal once in a while. And the little channel cats, those 2 to 4 pounders, are absolutely delicious, deep-fried and served with a mug of beer.

What's more, you don't have to shop at Lund's to taste bullheads and catfish. The waters around the Twin Cities are thick with

bullheads. As for catfish, the Minnesota, St. Croix and Mississippi Rivers may rank as three of the greatest catfish holes in the country.

Unfortunately, nobody brags about it.

Bullhead gear: Anything with a hook, line and sinker. Line size: baling twine to monofilament.

Catfish gear: Medium- to heavy-action rod with spin-cast, spinning or baitcasting reel. Line size: 8- to 17-pound test.

Bullhead baits: Worms, canned kernel corn, small dead minnows, nightcrawlers, doughballs, commercial stink bait, chicken livers.

Catfish baits: Minnows (dead or alive), cut-bait (minnow chunks), chicken liver, shrimp, doughballs, commercial stink bait.

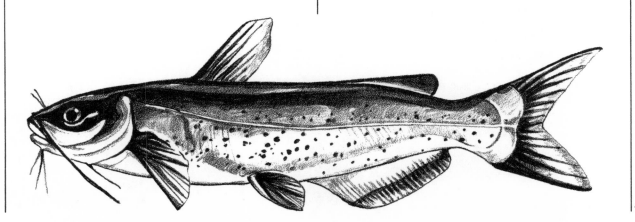

41

Catching city bullheads/

If you ever get skunked fishing bullheads, don't admit it. There isn't much a bullhead fisherman can do wrong. To catch a bullhead, bait up the hook and sink it to the bottom with a splitshot or lead sinker. And then wait. Won't be long before a bullhead will inhale whatever you're offering because there's hardly an acre of water in the Twin Cities that doesn't hold bullheads.

The trick is finding "hot spots" that harbor lunker bullheads of the 1-pound class.

Another trick is handling the fish after it's caught. The spines on the bullhead's fins are sharp. To get pricked is more frustrating than painful. I mean, you've caught this stupid fish and you can't even pick it up with any intelligence.

To be prepared for the frying pan, bullheads must be gutted and skinned, because the fish has no scales. Use a sharp knife and a pliers to peel the skin off.

The rest is the best. A skinned bullhead rolled in flour and deep fried is unbelievably tasty.

Best bullhead waters: Lake of the Isles, Independence, Rebecca, Bald Eagle, Marion.

Catching city catfish/

To catch a catfish, it helps to have insomnia. Catfish tend to be nocturnal feeders, which means the best fishing is usually at night. Sunrise and sunset also are good times.

The most common catfish species in Twin Cities waters is the bluish-colored channel cat. As its name implies, the channel cat thrives in rivers.

To locate channel cats, check out the river pools and deep cuts where the current is mild. River logjams also are catfish haunts.

One of my favorite catfishing methods is to stand on a sandbar above a river pool. Place the bait on a single or treble hook, add just enough lead weight to allow the bait to move along the bottom in the current. Unlike its bullhead cousin, a channel cat will often smack the bait with gusto. Feed line to the fish and then set the hook.

The best river catfishing usually starts in August when the river levels have dropped. The channel cats then normally congregate in the pools and deep-water cuts.

Catfishing is even more fun when on the sandbar there's a small campfire, a few hotdogs and a six-pack or two.

Best catfish waters: Minnesota River, St. Croix River, Mississippi River (below Coon Rapids Dam; mouth of Minnehaha Creek).

Twin Cities top 30 fishing spots/

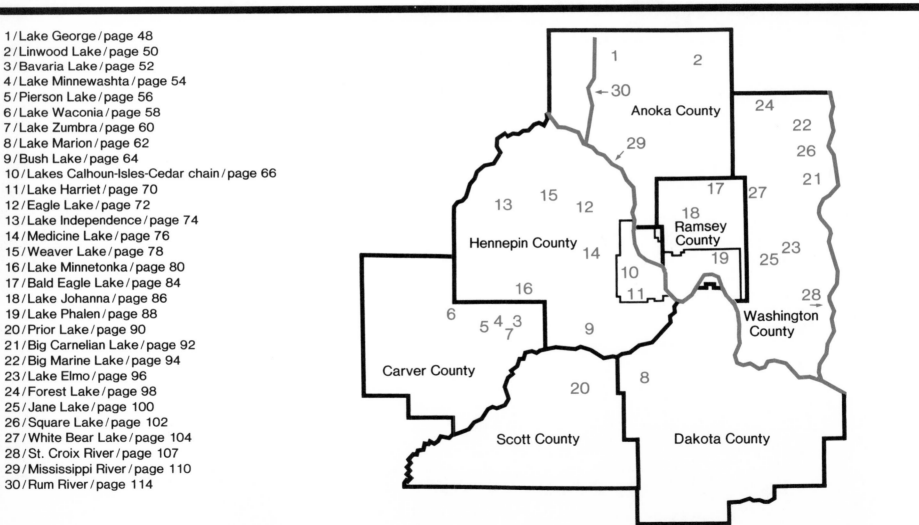

Anoka County

Hennepin County

Ramsey County

Washington County

Carver County

Scott County

Dakota County

Good fishing is where you find it.

Whether it's carp fishing below the I-494 bridge on the Mississippi or trout angling in Square Lake, fishing success is a matter of time, place, skill and—let's not forget—luck.

The place you choose to wet a line is an important part of the formula, of course. Goes without saying, you'll catch more fish in good lakes than in good storm sewers.

With that in mind, I've selected 30 top fishing spots out of some 200 lakes and rivers within the seven-county Twin Cities area. My top choices are not the only fishy waters in town. But they are fishing holes of repute and reliability.

You may note that a few fishing lakes with good reputations have been left off the list. There is a reason. Many lakes in the metro region are capable of harboring excellent fish populations but seldom do so on a consistent, year-after-year basis. The reason is our long winters that periodically cause winter fish-kills.

The lakes I've selected rarely suffer winter fish losses and all are accessible to the boating angler through public or fee boat-launch sites.

A word about boats. Undoubtedly, the han-diest fishing craft for the city lakes are the cartopper models or lightweight 14-foot fishing boats. An outboard of 10- to 15-horsepower is more than adequate on most of the metro waters. Fishermen with larger boats and motors will invariably have problems at some of the public access sites, which tend to be in shallow water areas.

A map of each lake or river is provided to show the public access sites, boat rentals and the lake depths. Every angler should learn how to read a depth map, the fisherman's "eyes" to the lake bottom. Remember that most fish like to be near something, such as weedlines, drop-offs, sunken islands, docks, rock piles, underwater points and so forth.

The depth maps will show you some of these fish haunts. Contour lines on a depth map indicate differences in depth by 5- or 10-foot intervals. If the contour lines are close together, it signifies a sharp drop in depth. Contour lines wide apart indicate a very gradual change in water depth. Circular contour lines indicating a shallow center with deeper water represent a sunken island or rock pile.

Depth maps of the city lakes are available for $2.25 each from the office of Public Documents, 117 University Av., St. Paul.

For a free listing of the mapped lakes, write to the Public Documents office. Or call toll free 1-800-652-9747.

The 30 fishing spots described here carry no guarantees of fishing success, of course.

Except one.

I'll guarantee that not one storm sewer made the list.

Lake George/

Size/
495 acres
Maximum depth/
32 feet
Water clarity/
good

Gamefish present/
northern pike
largemouth bass
bluegill
crappie
bowfin
bullhead

Public access/
east side
Fee access/
Tillburgs Resort, west side
Boat rental/
none

Lake George fishing tips/

Lake George is bowl-shaped mostly and the bowl is loaded with panfish of small sizes, northern pike of fair sizes and largemouth bass that can be line busters. The crappie count tends to be low.

Best way to fish Lake George is to troll or cast the weedline edges, some of which extend far into the lake. For that reason, weedless lures will be beneficial.

A shallow bay on the lake's south side may produce early spring action. Results are almost guaranteed for panfish but don't expect any whoppers.

Fisherman's advisory/
George Lake is a popular boating and waterskiing site on summer weekends. The public boat launch is shallow; launching large watercraft may be difficult.

Lake George/

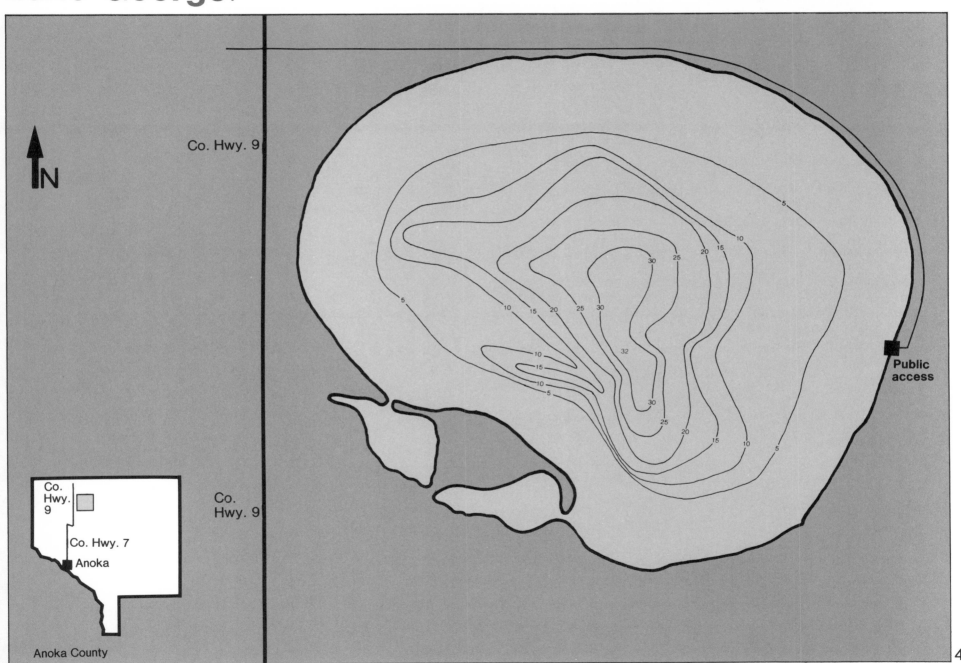

Co. Hwy. 9

N

5

5

10

10

15

15

20

20

25

25

30

30

32

10

15

10

5

25

20

15

10

5

30

Public access

Co.
Hwy.
9

Co. Hwy. 7

Anoka

Co.
Hwy. 9

Anoka County

Linwood Lake/

Size /
559 acres
Maximum depth /
42 Feet
Water clarity /
fair

Gamefish present /
northern pike   largemouth bass
walleye   bluegill
perch
white crappie
black crappie

Public access /
northwest shore
Fee access /
none
Boat rental /
Richard Werner residence,
phone 462-2070

Linwood Lake fishing tips/

Weedy bays and long underwater points are the best spots on Linwood Lake. Best fishing is for sunfish and crappies, which run from fair to good sizes. Expect anything, however. I was casting for crappies one rainy morning and ended up with a four-pound walleye on the end of the line.

Linwood may be a sleeper for bass since most fishing pressure is on panfish and northern pike.

Fisherman's advisory /
Early spring crappie fishing can be fast and furious. Summer weekend boating traffic is usually mild and bearable. Big-boat anglers will find the road approach to the public access is steep and the access, itself, is into shallow water.

Linwood Lake/

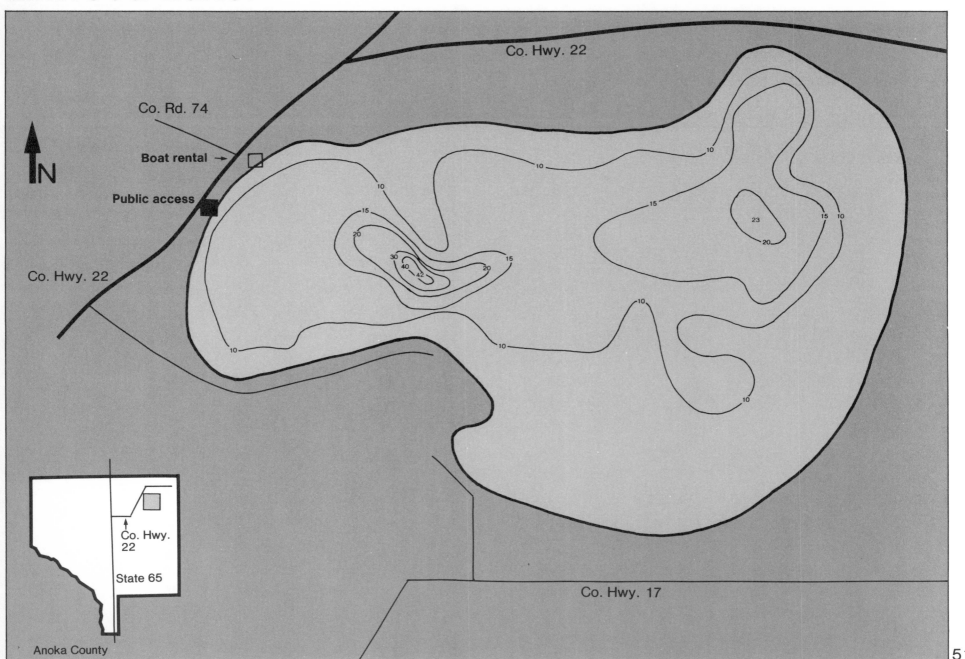

Co. Hwy. 22

Co. Rd. 74

Boat rental →

N

Public access

Co. Hwy. 22

10

15

20

30

40

42

20

15

10

10

10

15

23

20

15 10

10

10

Co. Hwy. 22

State 65

Co. Hwy. 17

Anoka County

Bavaria Lake/

Size/
200 acres
Maximum depth/
60 feet
Water clarity/
poor

Gamefish present/
northern pike
perch
sunfish
largemouth bass
black crappie
bullhead

Public access/
southwest shore
Fee access/
Schneider Shores Campground, east shore, summer phone 443-2726
Boat rentals/
none

Bavaria Lake fishing tips/

If northern pike is your desire and if you're not fussy about size, then this pretty lake is worth visiting. Northerns are plentiful and fairly fast-growing. The bluegills are also abundant but small. The lake's black crappies are of nice sizes but may be more difficult to find. May be a sleeper for largemouth bass. Most of the angling success occurs around the lake's perimeter on the outside edge of weedbeds and lily pads.

Bavaria Lake/

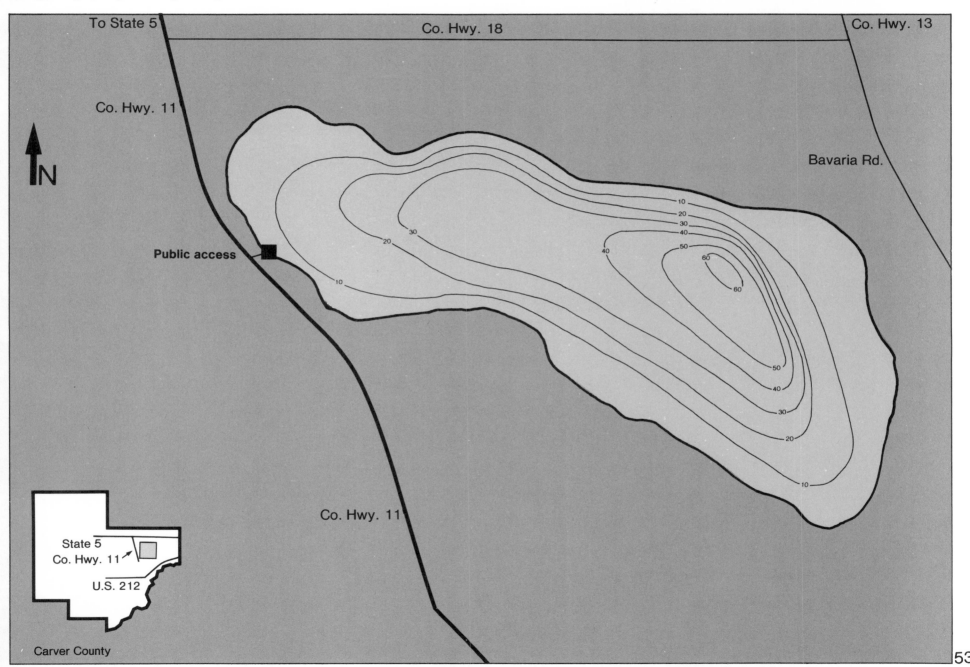

To State 5

Co. Hwy. 18

Co. Hwy. 13

Co. Hwy. 11

Bavaria Rd.

N

Public access

10
20
30
20
30
40
40
50
60
60
50
40
30
20
10
10

State 5
Co. Hwy. 11
U.S. 212

Co. Hwy. 11

Carver County

53

Lake Minnewashta/

Size /
742 acres
Maximum depth /
70 feet
Water clarity /
good

Gamefish present /
northern pike
sunfish
largemouth bass
bullhead
crappie

Public access /
east shore, 15-horsepower limit
Fee access /
Leach's Resort, west shore
Boat rentals /
Leach's Resort and Campground,
west shore, phone 474-8135.

Lake Minnewashta fishing tips /

An interesting lake with a variety of fishy-looking haunts. Minnewashta has a high northern pike population and nice-sized bluegills. Crappie numbers are low and few, if any, walleyes swim in Minnewashta. Largemouth-bass addicts may be in for a treat on Minnewashta. The lake by its close proximity to Minnetonka is often overlooked by bass enthusiasts. Minnewashta has produced bass lunkers of seven pounds.

Fisherman's advisory /
The public access may be unsuitable for launching bass boats and other heavy watercraft.

Lake Minnewashta/

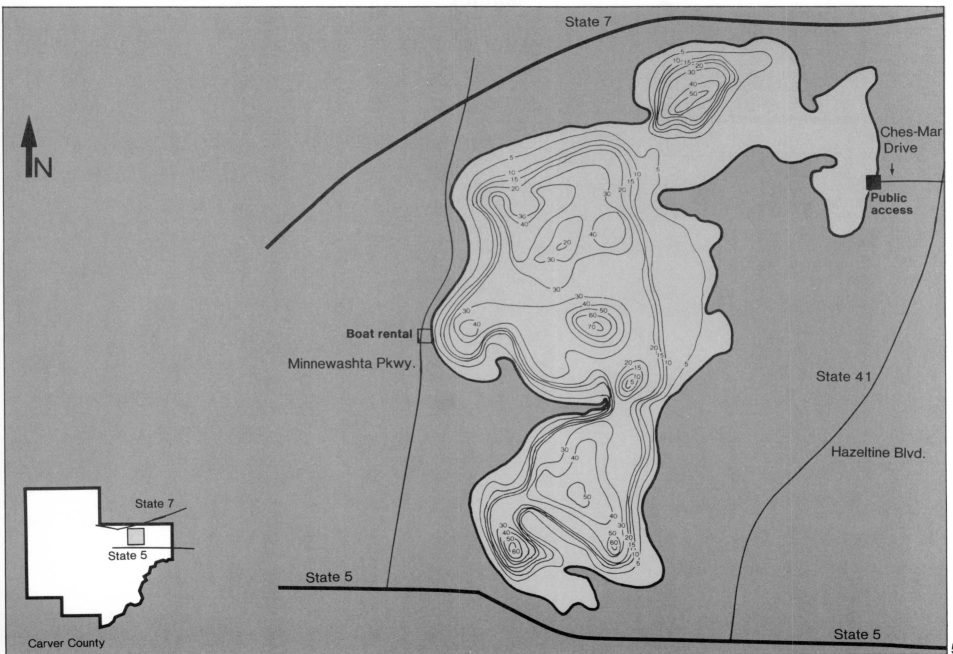

State 7

Ches-Mar Drive

Public access

N

Boat rental

Minnewashta Pkwy.

State 41

Hazeltine Blvd.

State 5

State 7

State 5

Carver County

Pierson Lake/

Size/
235 acres
Maximum depth/
40 feet
Water clarity/
good

Gamefish present/
largemouth bass
bluegill
northern pike
black crappie
bullhead
dogfish

Public access/
southwest shore
Fee access/
none
Boat rental/
none

Pierson Lake fishing tips/

The best tip is how to find the public access because the road leading to the boat launch is unmarked. Follow the Laketown Rd. south off of Hwy. 5 west of Victoria. Watch for the Laketown Township Hall and take the first left on a unnamed gravel road where you see three Minneapolis Tribune delivery tubes. Pierson is worth looking for. Good populations of northern pike, bluegills, crappies and largemouth bass swim in its waters. Walleyes are rare but usually large. Crappies are abundant although the size is generally small.

Pierson Lake/

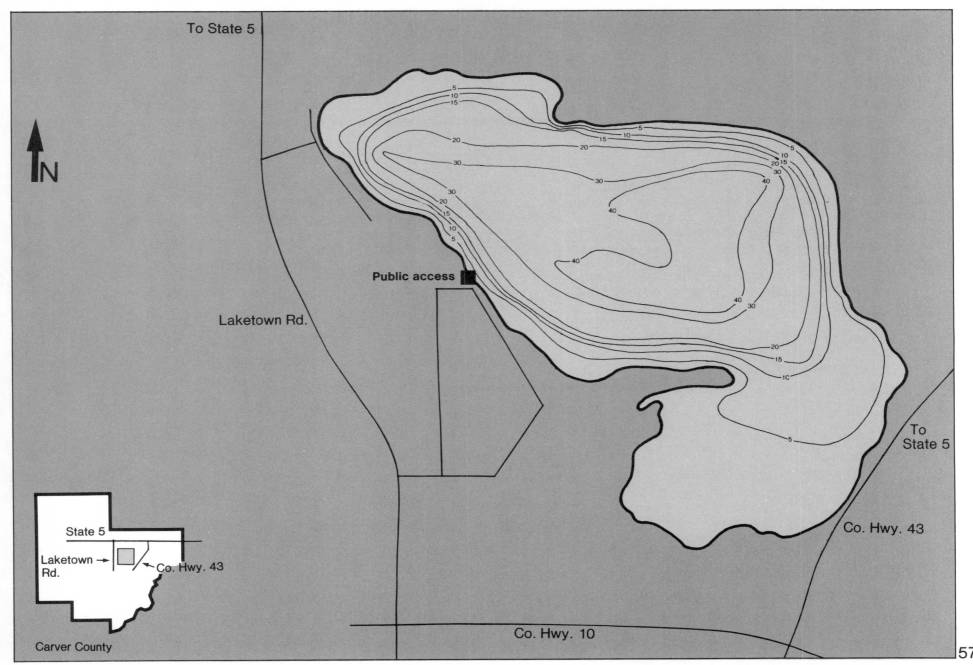

To State 5

N

Public access

Laketown Rd.

To State 5

Co. Hwy. 43

State 5

Laketown Rd.

Co. Hwy. 43

Carver County

Co. Hwy. 10

Lake Waconia/

Size/
3,104 acres
Maximum depth/
37 feet
Water clarity/
poor

Gamefish present/
largemouth bass	bluegill
walleye	bullhead
northern pike	
sheepshead	
crappie	

Public access/
east shore
Fee access/
Intown Marine, south shore; Waconia Marine, south shore
Boat rental/
Intown Marine, south shore, phone 442-2096;
Waconia Marine, south shore, phone 442-2820

Lake Waconia fishing tips/

Waconia can be a real honey hole for anglers of any ilk. Trophy walleyes, northern pike, bass and excellent panfishing are possible on Waconia. The key to success is finding and fishing the lake's many humps or reefs, which attract fish. These humps are difficult to find without the aid of an electronic depth finder, although local bait shops sell lake maps that provide shore markings to the best fish-producing spots. The shallow, weedy bays of Waconia should not be overlooked for bass and northern pike.

If you hook a hefty fish in Waconia, don't get too excited until you see what's on the end of the line. Your expected trophy could turn out to be a sheepshead, a fish species that nobody brags about catching.

For best results on Waconia, plan to use live bait.

Fisherman's advisory/
On windy days Waconia can become hazardous to boaters because of its size and amount of open water.

Lake Waconia/

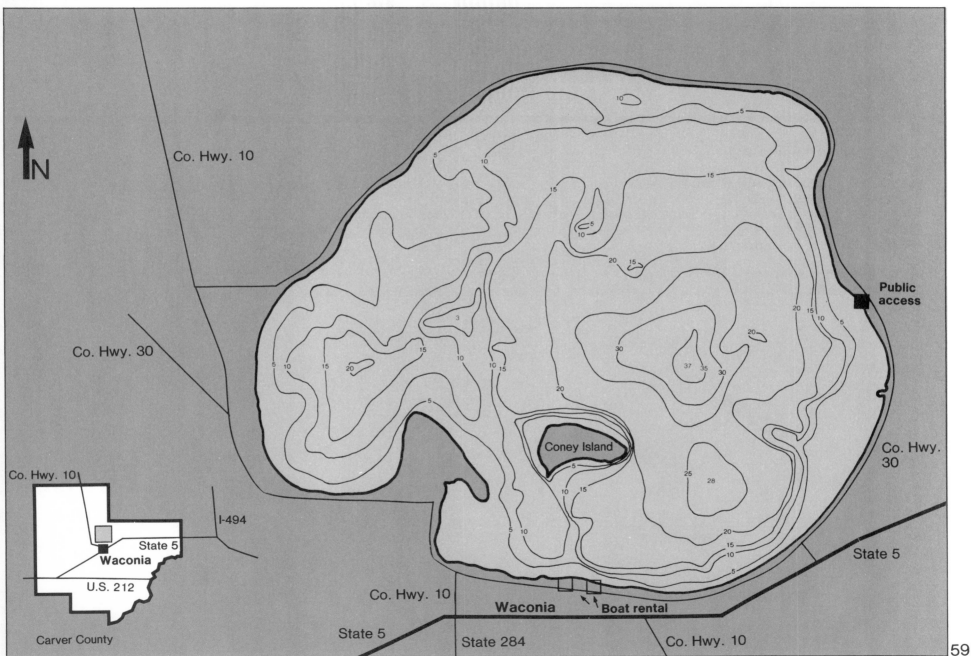

N

Co. Hwy. 10

Co. Hwy. 30

Co. Hwy. 10

I-494

State 5

Waconia

U.S. 212

Carver County

Public access

Co. Hwy. 30

State 5

Coney Island

Co. Hwy. 10

Waconia

Boat rental

State 5

State 284

Co. Hwy. 10

59

Lake Zumbra/

Size/
162 acres
Maximum depth/
58 feet
Water clarity/
fair

Gamefish present/
northern pike
largemouth bass
crappie
bluegill
perch

Public access/
south shore
Fee access/
none
Boat rentals/
none

Lake Zumbra fishing tips/

A fun lake if catching northern pike and largemouth bass is what makes you smile. The northerns are relatively abundant and the bass are of hefty sizes, up to five pounds or more. Zumbra has extensive fields of lilypads and shallow weedbeds. Most of the fishing action will come from these areas, which means go to Zumbra with an assortment of weedless lures. High populations of crappies and bluegills are available but their sizes are small.

Fisherman's advisory/
The public launch is in extremely shallow water. Shore fishing access is available along Hwy. 7, which runs along the north end of Zumbra.

Lake Zumbra/

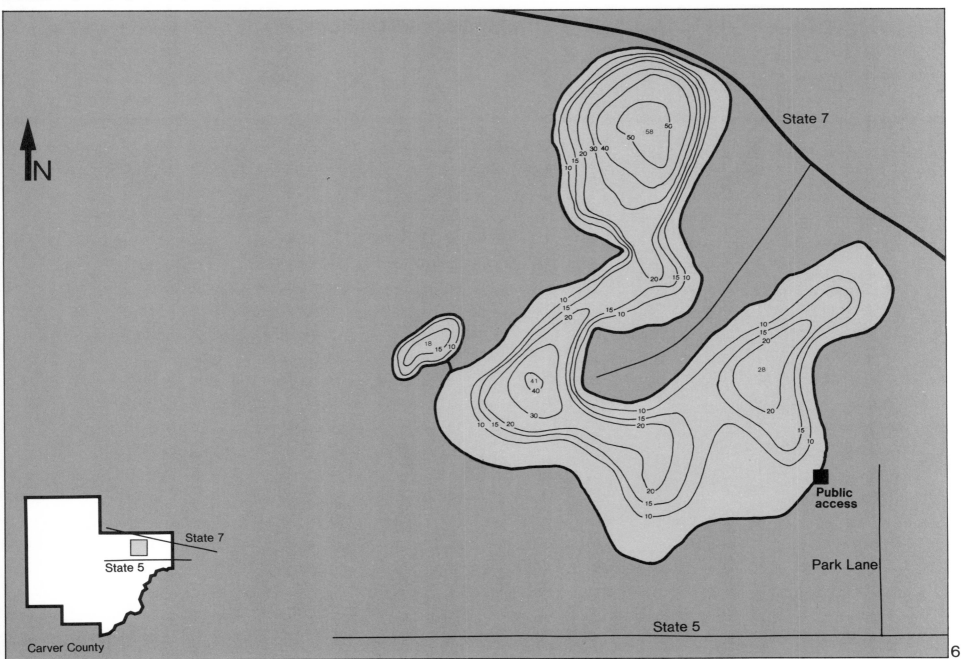

State 7

State 7

State 5

Public access

Park Lane

State 5

Carver County

58
50
50
40 30 20
15
10
20 15 10
18 15 10
10 15 20
15 10
10 15 20
10 15 20
41 40
30
10 15 20
28
20
15 10
10 15 20
20 15 10

N

Lake Marion/

Size/
560 acres
Maximum depth/
21 feet
Water clarity/
fair

Gamefish present/
largemouth bass
crappie
northern pike
perch
bullhead
walleye

Public access/
west shore
Fee access/
southeast shore, launch free, parking fee
Boat rental/
none

Lake Marion fishing tips/

Lake Marion has hefty fish. Largemouth bass are moderately abundant but sizes run in the 4-pound category. Trophy size northern pike of 10 pounds or better also swim in the waters. Lake Marion has a high population of bluegills but sizes run small. Large bullheads also are present. Most of the fishing action is along the weedline drop-offs and underwater points. Walleyes have been stocked in Lake Marion but the walleye action usually is poor.

Fisherman's advisory/
Large fishing boats may be difficult to launch on the west shore public access which has a shallow, natural sand ramp.

Lake Marion/

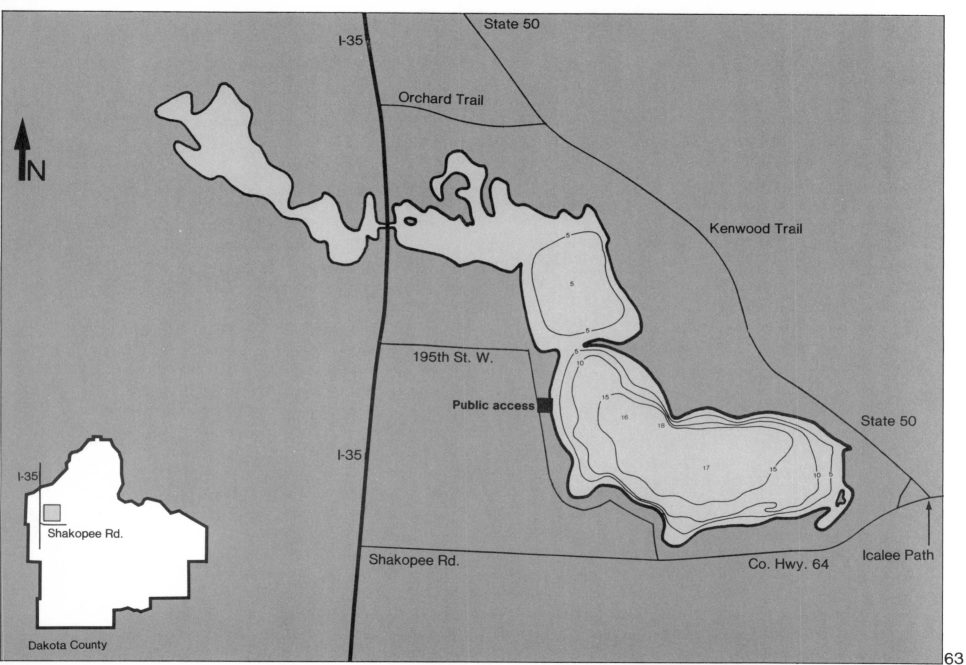

State 50

I-35

Orchard Trail

Kenwood Trail

N

5

5

5

5

195th St. W.

10

Public access

15

16

18

17

15

10

5

State 50

I-35

Shakopee Rd.

Co. Hwy. 64

Icalee Path

I-35

Shakopee Rd.

Dakota County

Bush Lake/

Size/
192 acres
Maximum depth/
28 feet
Water clarity/
excellent

Gamefish present/
northern pike
largemouth bass
black crappie
bluegill
perch
bullhead

Public access/
east shore, limited to 6-horsepower
outboard motors
Fee access/
none
Boat rental/
none

Bush Lake fishing tips/

Surrounded by Bloomington park land, Bush Lake long has been known for its lunker largemouth bass of six pounds or more. Shallow weed bays and weedline drop-offs provide the bass habitat, so come equipped with weedless lures. Bush also harbors a high population of northern pike and bluegills but both tend to run small. The crappie count is low.

Bush Lake/

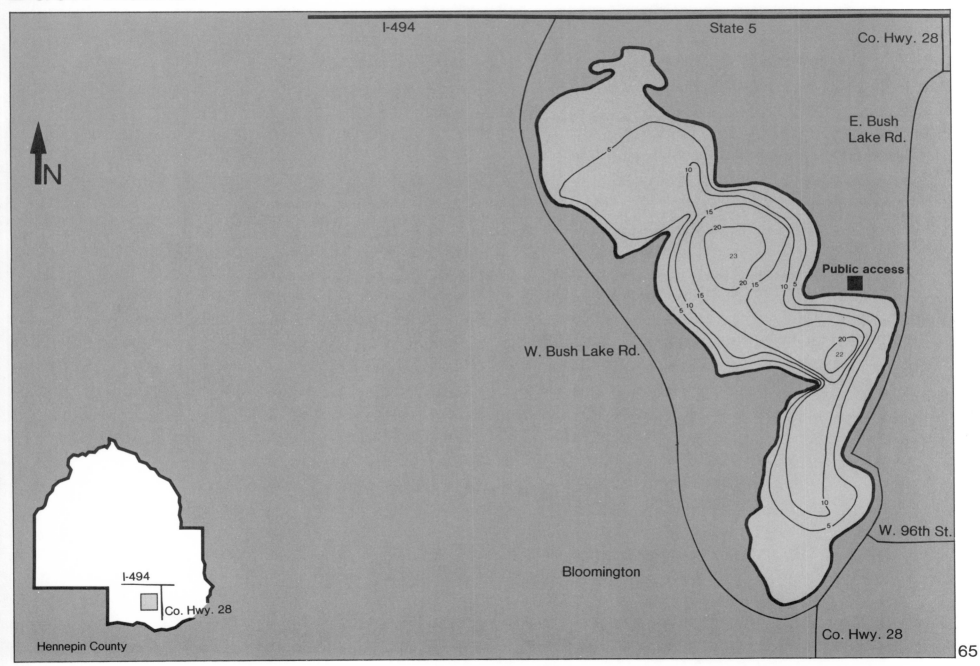

I-494

State 5

Co. Hwy. 28

E. Bush
Lake Rd.

N

5

10

15

20

23

20 15

15

5 10

20 15 10 5

Public access

20

22

W. Bush Lake Rd.

10

5

W. 96th St.

Bloomington

I-494

Co. Hwy. 28

Hennepin County

Co. Hwy. 28

65

Lakes Calhoun-Isles-Cedar Chain/

Size/
Calhoun, 518 acres; Isle, 109; Cedar, 168
Maximum depth/
Calhoun, 90 feet; Isles, 31 feet; Cedar, 51 feet.
Water clarity/
Calhoun, fair; Isles, poor; Cedar, fair

Gamefish present/
largemouth bass   bluegill
northern pike   perch
walleye   (Same species in all three lakes).
bullhead
crappie

Public access/
northeast shore of Lake Calhoun
Fee access/
none
Boat rental/
canoes only, Minneapolis Park Board; motor permits required, phone 348-5406

Lakes Calhoun, Isles and Cedar fishing tips/

Although the three lakes are connected by channels, each lake requires a different fishing approach. The best fishing in Calhoun is near the lake's long, weedy underwater points and along the edge of aquatic vegetation that rings most of the shoreline. On Lake of the Isles, weedy underwater flats next to deep water are the best places. Cedar has a mixture of weedy underwater points, lily pad beds and a sunken island or two.

Panfish in all three lakes tend to be small. But more than one fisherman has been surprised by the size of the northern pike and largemouth bass that are hauled from these inner city waters.

Fisherman's advisory/
Weekend canoe traffic is heavy in summer.

Lake Calhoun/

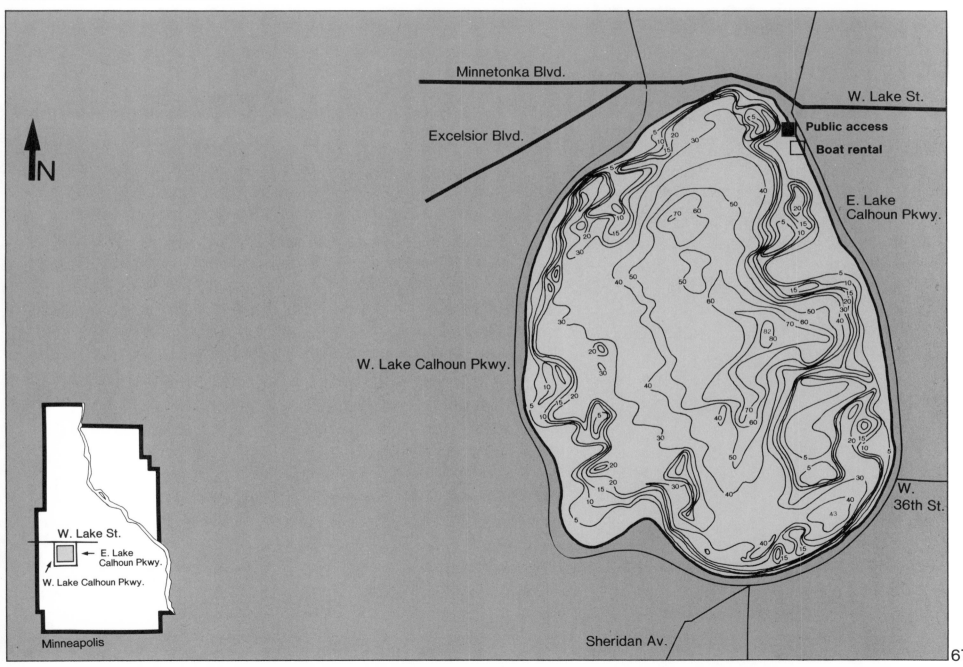

Minnetonka Blvd.

W. Lake St.

Excelsior Blvd.

Public access

Boat rental

E. Lake
Calhoun Pkwy.

N

W. Lake Calhoun Pkwy.

W.
36th St.

Minneapolis

W. Lake St.

E. Lake
Calhoun Pkwy.

W. Lake Calhoun Pkwy.

Sheridan Av.

Lake of the Isles/

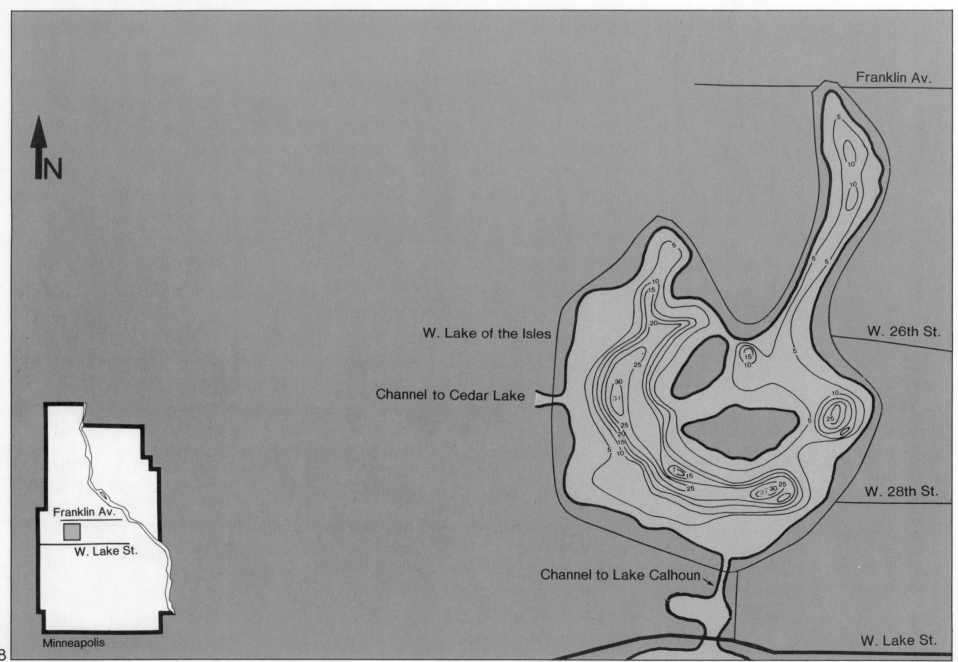

Franklin Av.

W. 26th St.

W. Lake of the Isles

Channel to Cedar Lake

W. 28th St.

Channel to Lake Calhoun

W. Lake St.

Franklin Av.

W. Lake St.

Minneapolis

Cedar Lake/

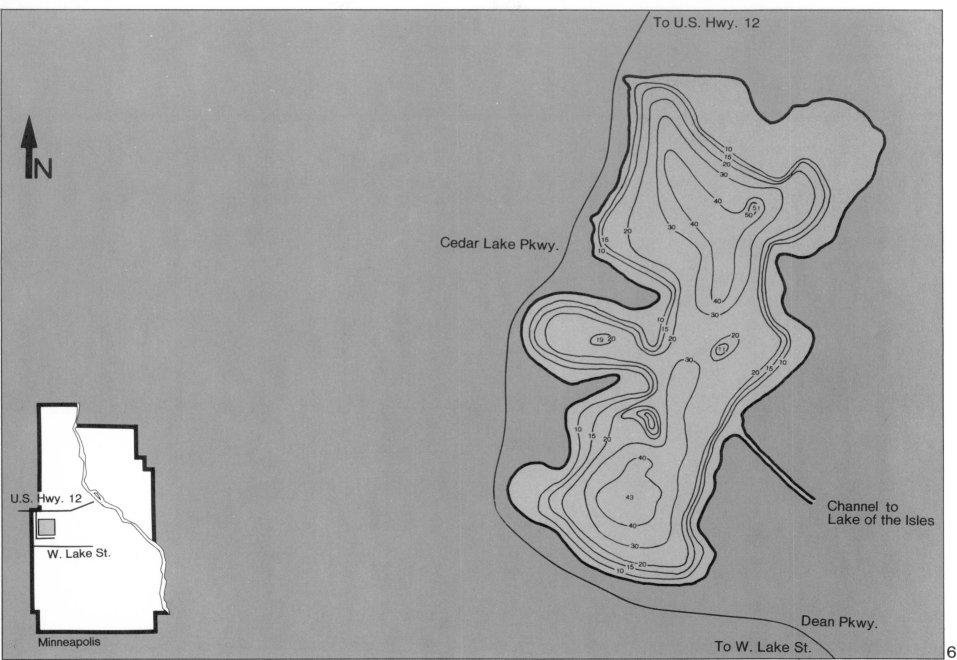

N

To U.S. Hwy. 12

Cedar Lake Pkwy.

10
15
20
30
40
51
50
40
40
20
15
10
30
40
30
10
15
20
19 20
20
11
30
20 15 10
10 15 20
40
43
40
30
10 15 20

Channel to
Lake of the Isles

Dean Pkwy.

To W. Lake St.

U.S. Hwy. 12

W. Lake St.

Minneapolis

Lake Harriet/

Size/
345 acres
Maximum depth/
82 feet
Water clarity/
fair

Gamefish present/
walleye   northern pike
muskellunge   largemouth bass
crappies
perch
bluegill

Public access/
northwest shore
Fee access/
none
Boat rental/
none

Lake Harriet fishing tips/

Harriet may be surrounded by joggers and dotted with sailboats. But the lake also is loaded with walleyes up to 10 pounds or more. But that's not all. Legal-sized muskies (more than 30 inches in length) also roam in Harriet. Best fishing spots are the gradual drop-offs into deep water and underwater points. Weedbeds may or may not be present. Largemouth bass and northern pike are not common. Crappies and bluegills are fair.

Lake Harriet/

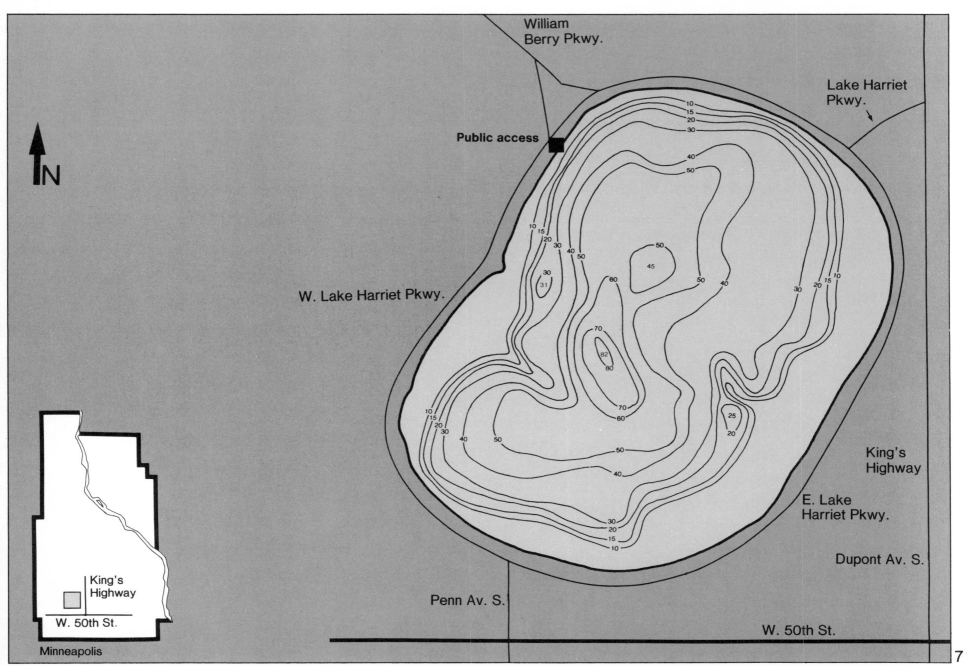

William Berry Pkwy.

Lake Harriet Pkwy.

Public access

W. Lake Harriet Pkwy.

King's Highway

E. Lake Harriet Pkwy.

Dupont Av. S.

Penn Av. S.

W. 50th St.

King's Highway

W. 50th St.

Minneapolis

N

Eagle Lake/

Size/
290 acres
Maximum depth/
34 feet
Water clarity/
poor

Gamefish present/
largemouth bass
northern pike
bluegill
black crappie
walleye
bullhead

Public access/
northeast shore
Fee access/
None
Boat rental/
Lenarz Resort, east shore, phone 535-1393

Eagle Lake fishing tips/

If you're looking to catch northern pike, Eagle is the right place. A high pike population and inviting weedbeds make the game interesting. A jig and minnow combination should produce. Bluegills and crappies are plentiful but of average size. Eagle could also be a sleeper for trophy largemouth bass. That is, if you can keep the northern pike from hitting.

Eagle Lake/

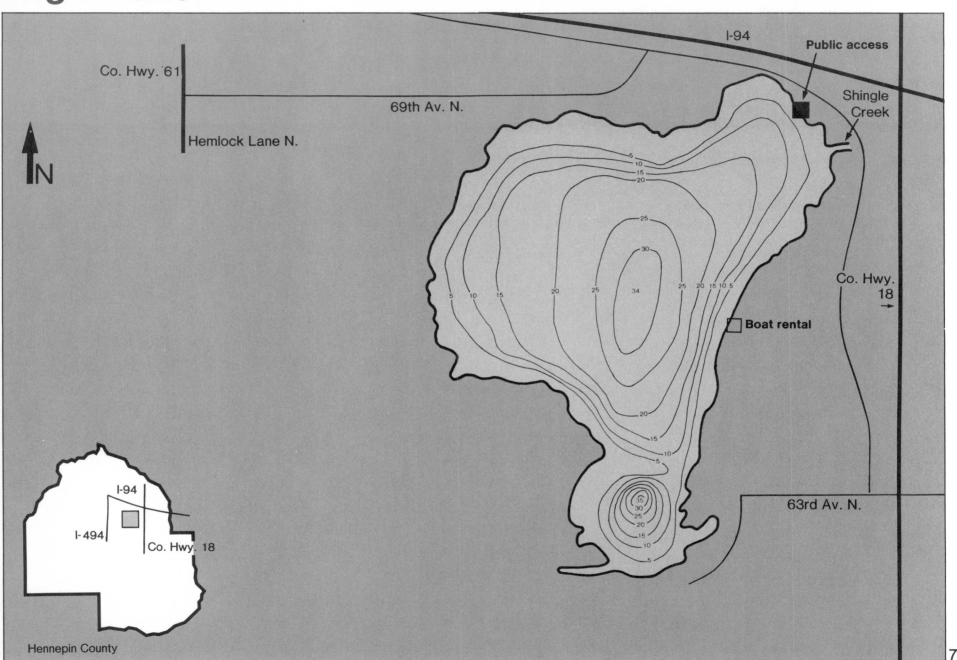

I-94

Public access

Co. Hwy. 61

69th Av. N.

Shingle Creek

Hemlock Lane N.

N

5
10
15
20

25

30

34

Co. Hwy. 18

Boat rental

5 10 15 20 25 34 25 20 15 10 5

20

15

10

5

35
30
25
20
15
10
5

63rd Av. N.

I-94

I-494

Co. Hwy. 18

Hennepin County

Lake Independence/

Size /
844 acres
Maximum depth /
58 feet
Water clarity /
poor

Gamefish present /
northern pike	bluegill
muskellunge	crappie
largemouth bass	
walleye	
bullhead	

Public access /
east shore in Baker Park Reserve
Fee access /
None
Boat rental /
None

Lake Independence fishing tips /

The largest muskies in the Twin Cities roam in Lake Independence. Cast the shallow, weedy flats to find them. A high population of hefty northern pike also is present. Crappies and bluegills are above average size. Walleye catches are rare. Because of the lake's murky waters, best fishing likely will be in less than 15 feet of water.

Fisherman's advisory /
Weekend boating traffic can be heavy.

Lake Independence/

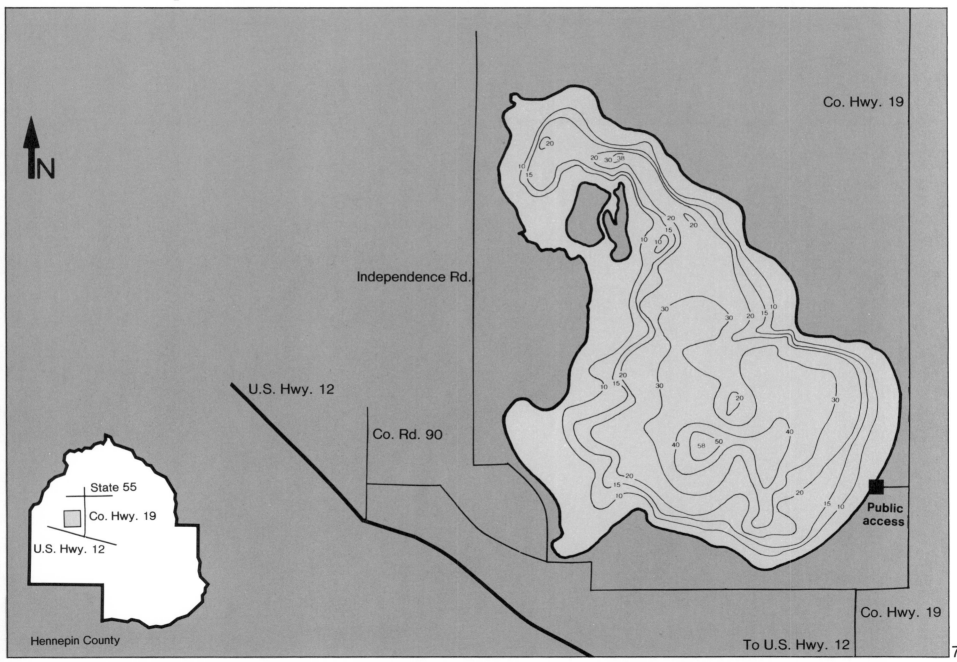

Co. Hwy. 19

Independence Rd.

U.S. Hwy. 12

Co. Rd. 90

20

20 30 38

10
15

20

20

15

10 10

30

30 20 15

10

20

10 15

30

20

40

40

58 50

20

15

10

20

15 10

**Public
access**

State 55

Co. Hwy. 19

U.S. Hwy. 12

Hennepin County

Co. Hwy. 19

To U.S. Hwy. 12

75

Medicine Lake/

Size/
885 acres
Maximum depth/
49 feet
Water clarity/
fair

Gamefish present/
northern pike
bluegill
crappie
largemouth bass
perch

Public access/
North shore (summer of 1982)
Fee access/
None

Boat rental/
Medicine Lake Boat Rental, 2900 E. Medicine Lake Blvd., 546–3849; Harty's Boat and Bait, 1920 Medicine Lake Blvd., 546–3849

Medicine Lake fishing tips/

Check out the long points and deep-water drop-offs along the lake's weedlines. These are the haunts of northern pike and largemouth bass. Medicine Lake, the second largest lake in the Twin Cities area, has a good supply of both species. Crappies and bluegills also are abundant but tend to run small. Best panfishing is in winter. The fishing on Medicine might be slow when it rains, too. A kid on a Medicine Lake dock once told me the fish eat the raindrops.

Medicine Lake/

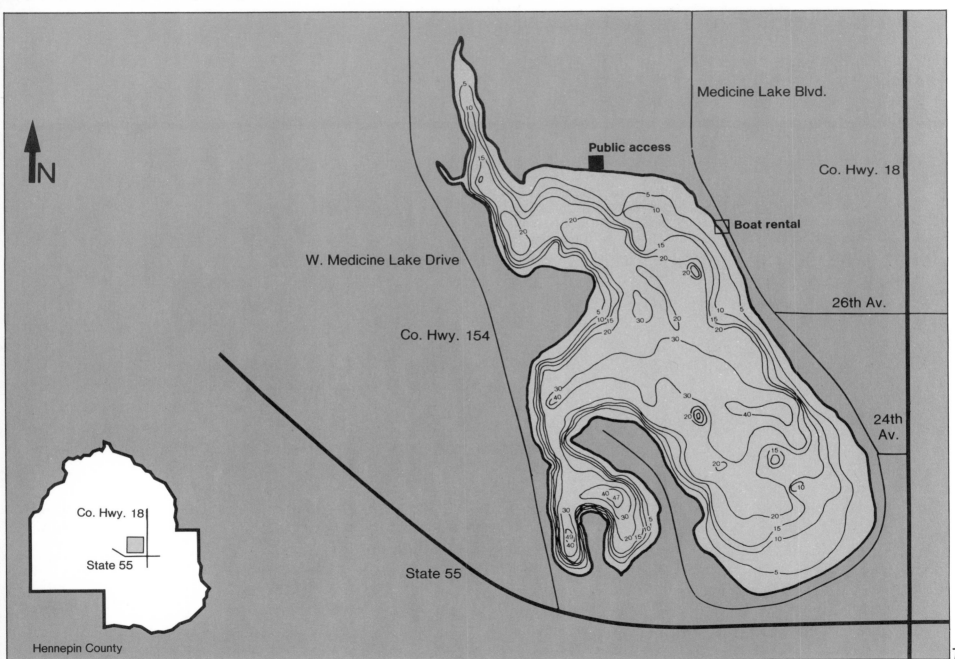

N

Medicine Lake Blvd.

Public access

Co. Hwy. 18

Boat rental

W. Medicine Lake Drive

26th Av.

Co. Hwy. 154

24th Av.

Co. Hwy. 18

State 55

State 55

Hennepin County

Weaver Lake/

Size /
149 acres
Maximum depth /
57 feet
Water clarity /
good

Gamefish present /
largemouth bass
northern pike
bluegill
crappie
bullhead

Public access /
northwest shore
Fee access /
none
Boat rental /
none

Weaver Lake fishing tips /

Weaver is a plain, bowl-shaped lake but don't be misled. Large numbers of northern pike and largemouth bass swim in Weaver. The best fishing will be found almost exclusively along the underwater weedline, which extends to depths of about 12 feet. Lilypad beds on the lake's south shore also hold fish. Bluegills are plentiful; crappie numbers are low. Trophy northern pike are possible and the largemouth bass can be hefty 4- to 5-pounders. Ideal lake for trolling artificial lures and casting plastic worms.

Weaver Lake/

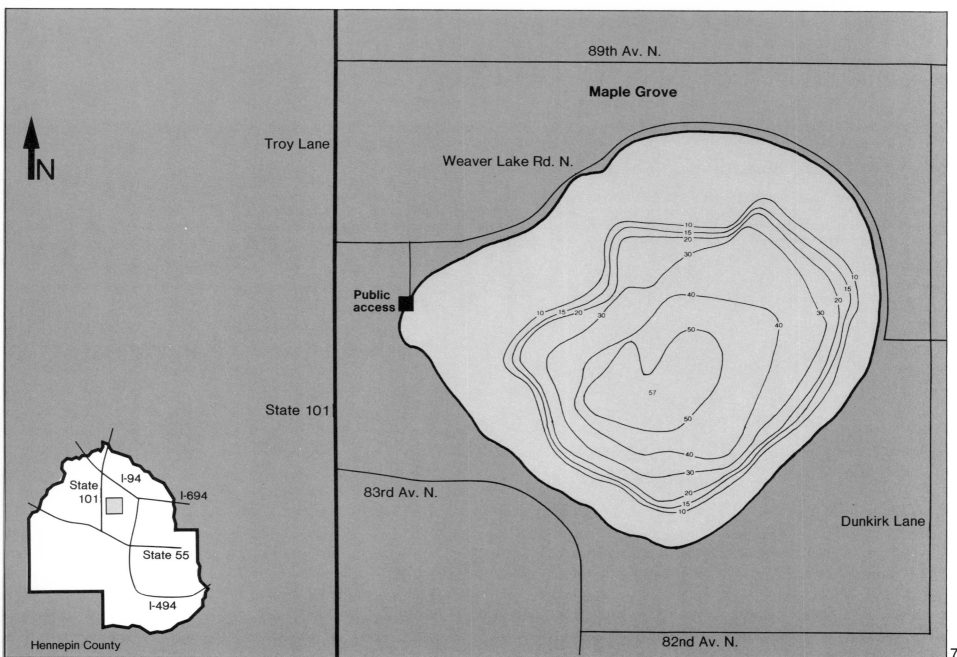

N

89th Av. N.

Maple Grove

Troy Lane

Weaver Lake Rd. N.

Public access

State 101

83rd Av. N.

Dunkirk Lane

82nd Av. N.

I-94

State 101

I-694

State 55

I-494

Hennepin County

Lake Minnetonka/

Size/
14,528 acres
Maximum depth/
113 feet
Water clarity/
good

Gamefish present/

largemouth bass	bluegill
walleye	perch
northern pike	smallmouth bass
muskellunge	bullhead
white crappie	rock bass
black crappie	

Public access/
Wayzata Bay, Gray's Bay (2), North Arm, Spring Park Bay; Phelps Bay, Halsted's Bay.
Fee access/
Deephaven Municipal, Carson's Bay; Tonka Bay Marina, Excelsior; Boat and Motor Mart, St. Alban's Bay; Greenwood Marina, St. Alban's Bay; Minnetonka Boat Works, Carson's Bay; Seashore Condo, Jennings Bay; Rockvam Boat Works, Lower West Arm; Gayle's Marina, Maxwell Bay; Northstar Marina, Maxwell Bay; Howard's Point Resort, Smithtown Bay; Gray's Bay Marina, Gray's Bay.

Boat Rental/
Paul's Landing, Smith Bay, phone 473-0281; Gray's Bay Marina, Gray's Bay, phone 473-2550; Howard's Point Resort, Smithtown Bay, phone 474-9982; Martin's and Sons, Harrison's Bay, 472-1220.

Lake Minnetonka/

Lake Minnetonka fishing tips/

Whatever you desire to catch, Minnetonka has it. Despite the lake's size, keep in mind that each bay is a lake within itself. Concentrate your fishing on one bay at a time. Minnetonka also is unique because almost every underwater point is marked with a boating navigation buoy. These points will hold bass, northern pike, crappies, smallmouth bass and muskies. Elsewhere, fish the underwater weedlines which vary in depth from bay to bay.

Minnetonka also has extensive fields of lilypads and shallow weedy bays that hold fish. Most of the walleyes and smallmouth bass are found in Smith, Brown's and Wayzata Bays. Bluegills and crappies are found throughout the lake's 114 miles of shoreline. But the best panfish bays are Spring Park, Carmen's, Phelps, Forest Lake and Halsted's.

Minnetonka, the largest of the city lakes, is famed for its largemouth bass fishing. For good reason. The largemouth are found in every bay on the lake, in weedbeds and under boat docks. Northern pike also are abundant but the best bays are West Arm, North Arm, Spring Park, Echo. The muskie population is scattered among the lake's many weedy haunts. But there're enough of the toothy fish to make Minnetonka a legitimate muskie fishing lake. Good stringers of walleyes are increasingly common because of heavy stocking by the Department of Natural Resources.

In summary, if you can't decide on what lake to fish, you'll never make a mistake trying Minnetonka.

Fisherman's advisory/
Minnetonka boat traffic on weekends is extremely heavy during midday hours.

Lake Minnetonka/

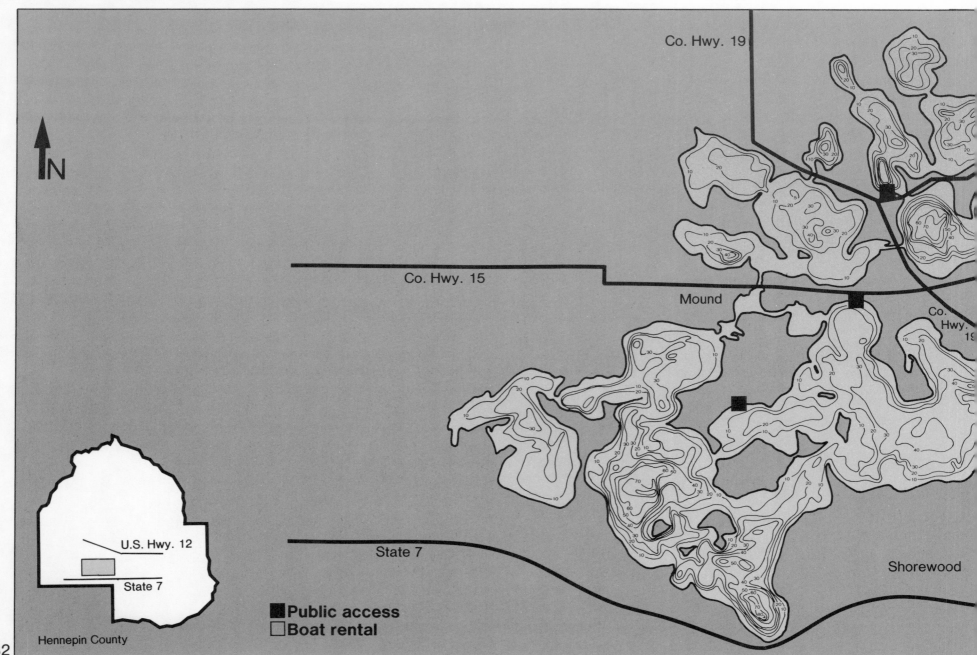

Co. Hwy. 19

Co. Hwy. 15

Mound

Co. Hwy. 19

State 7

Shorewood

U.S. Hwy. 12

State 7

Hennepin County

■ Public access
☐ Boat rental

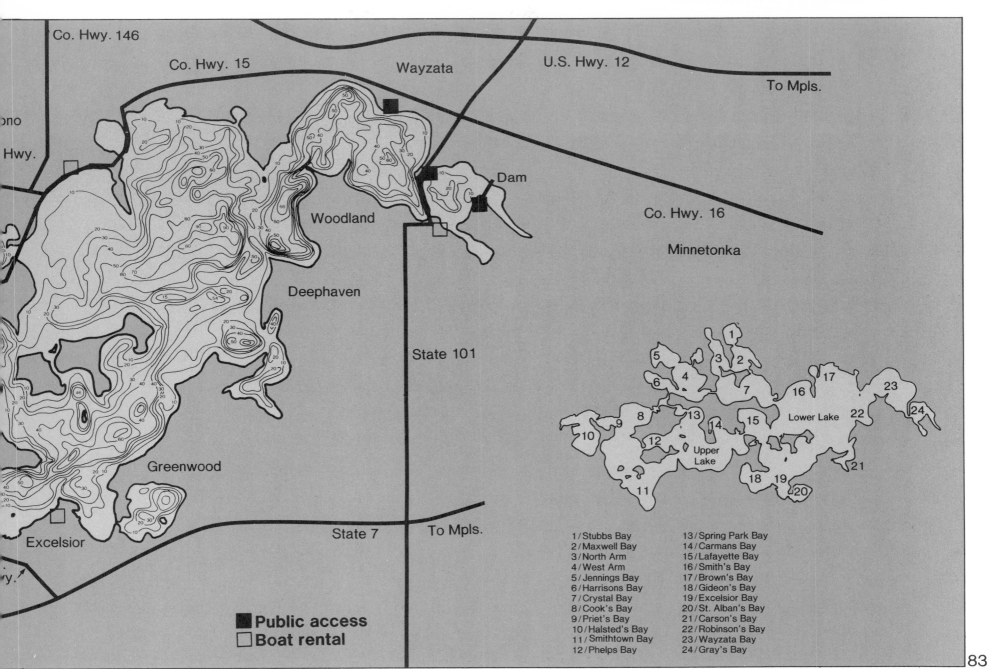

Co. Hwy. 146

Co. Hwy. 15

Wayzata

U.S. Hwy. 12

To Mpls.

ono

Hwy.

Dam

Co. Hwy. 16

Woodland

Minnetonka

Deephaven

State 101

Greenwood

Excelsior

State 7

To Mpls.

■ Public access
□ Boat rental

Lower Lake

Upper Lake

1 / Stubbs Bay	13 / Spring Park Bay
2 / Maxwell Bay	14 / Carmans Bay
3 / North Arm	15 / Lafayette Bay
4 / West Arm	16 / Smith's Bay
5 / Jennings Bay	17 / Brown's Bay
6 / Harrisons Bay	18 / Gideon's Bay
7 / Crystal Bay	19 / Excelsior Bay
8 / Cook's Bay	20 / St. Alban's Bay
9 / Priet's Bay	21 / Carson's Bay
10 / Halsted's Bay	22 / Robinson's Bay
11 / Smithtown Bay	23 / Wayzata Bay
12 / Phelps Bay	24 / Gray's Bay

83

Bald Eagle Lake/

Size/
1,012 acres
Maximum depth/
39 feet
Water clarity/
poor

Gamefish present/
northern pike
perch
largemouth bass
bluegill
crappie
bullheads

Public access/
east shore
Fee access/
none
Boat rental/
none

Bald Eagle fishing tips/

Despite its reputation as a popular waterskiing lake, Bald Eagle also harbors action below the surface. A hefty supply of crappies, bluegills and northern pike swim in Bald Eagle. Because of the lake's murky water, the weedbeds rarely extend deeper than six feet. Best fishing action will be found on the outside edge of the weedbeds or near the lilypad fields in the bays. To catch northern pike, troll the outside of the weedbeds. Lunker largemouth bass also roam in the weedy shallows. Cast close to shore.

Fisherman's advisory/
Expect heavy boating traffic on hot, summer weekends. Excellent public launch for boats of all sizes.

Bald Eagle Lake/

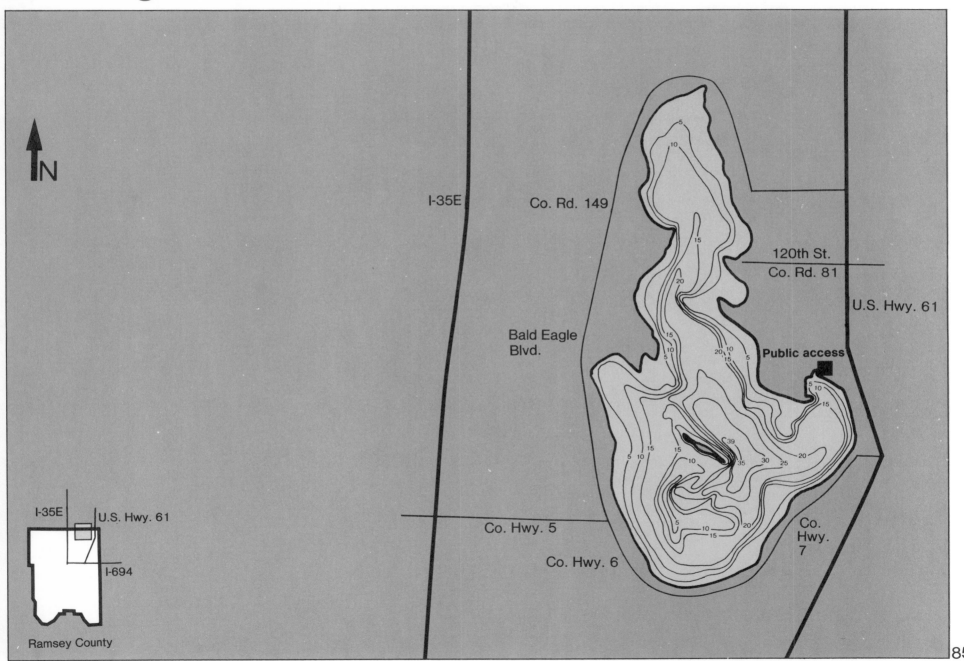

N

I-35E

Co. Rd. 149

120th St.
Co. Rd. 81

U.S. Hwy. 61

Bald Eagle
Blvd.

Public access

Co. Hwy. 5

Co.
Hwy.
7

Co. Hwy. 6

I-35E   U.S. Hwy. 61

I-694

Ramsey County

Lake Johanna/

Size/
200 acres
Maximum depth/
41 feet
Water clarity/
fair

Gamefish present/
northern pike   crappie
largemouth bass   bluegill
perch
walleye
bullhead

Public access/
north shore
Fee access/
none
Boat rental/
none

Lake Johanna fishing tips/

Bass fishermen will get a kick and maybe even a lunker out of Johanna. Although surrounded by private homes, the lake produces fine largemouth bass. Sunken islands and weedy points are best spots. But don't overlook the private boat docks. Plastic worms, diving plugs and spinnerbaits will work on Johanna bass. Northern pike and crappie populations also are good. The bluegills are abundant but of small size. Walleyes are rare.

Fisherman's advisory/
Heavy boat traffic on weekends. Public launch is excellent for boats of all sizes.

Lake Johanna/

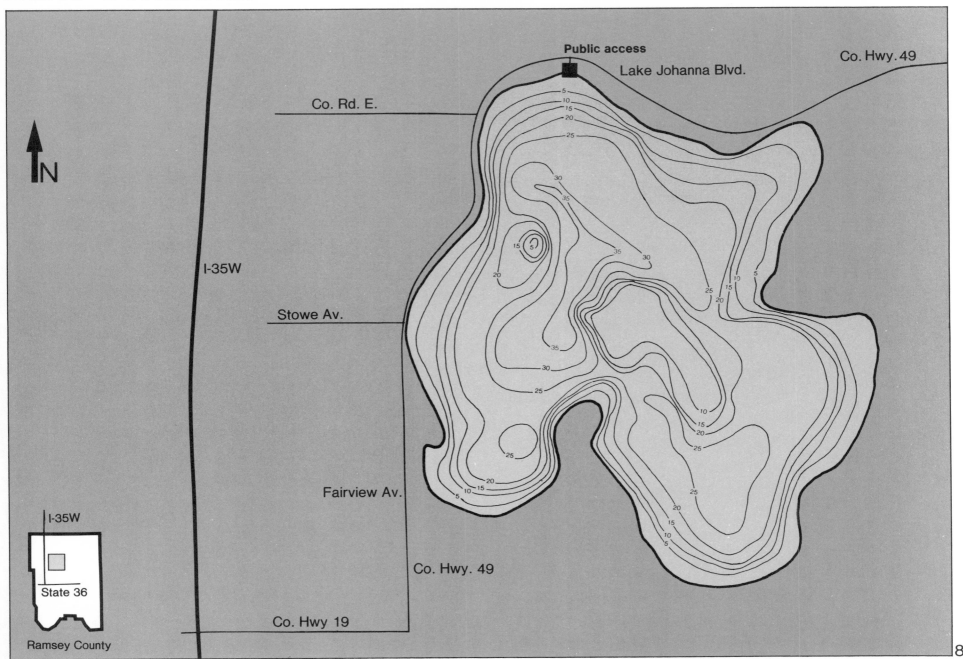

Public access

Lake Johanna Blvd.

Co. Hwy. 49

Co. Rd. E.

N

I-35W

Stowe Av.

5
10
15
20
25
30
35
35
30
25
20
15
5
10
15
20
25
30
35
35
30
25
10
15
20
25
25
20
15
10
5
25
20
15
10
5

Fairview Av.

Co. Hwy. 49

I-35W

State 36

Ramsey County

Co. Hwy 19

Lake Phalen/

Size /
198 acres
Maximum depth /
91 feet
Water clarity /
excellent

Gamefish present /
largemouth bass
walleyes
crappie
perch
bluegill
bullhead

Public access /
west shore
Fee access /
none
Boat rental /
canoes only, Phalen Park, phone 774-9759.

Lake Phalen fishing tips /

It looks like a typical city lake in a city park, surrounded by boulevards and manicured lawns. But don't be misled. Lake Phalen has a high population of walleyes. Yes, walleyes, which were stocked in the lake by DNR. Also abundant are largemouth bass, bluegills and northern pike. The bass tend to run small but the bluegills often are more than pan-sized. Crappie count is fair.

Fisherman's advisory /
Excellent shore-fishing opportunities. Public land surrounds most of the lake. Only electric trolling motors are permitted.

Lake Phalen/

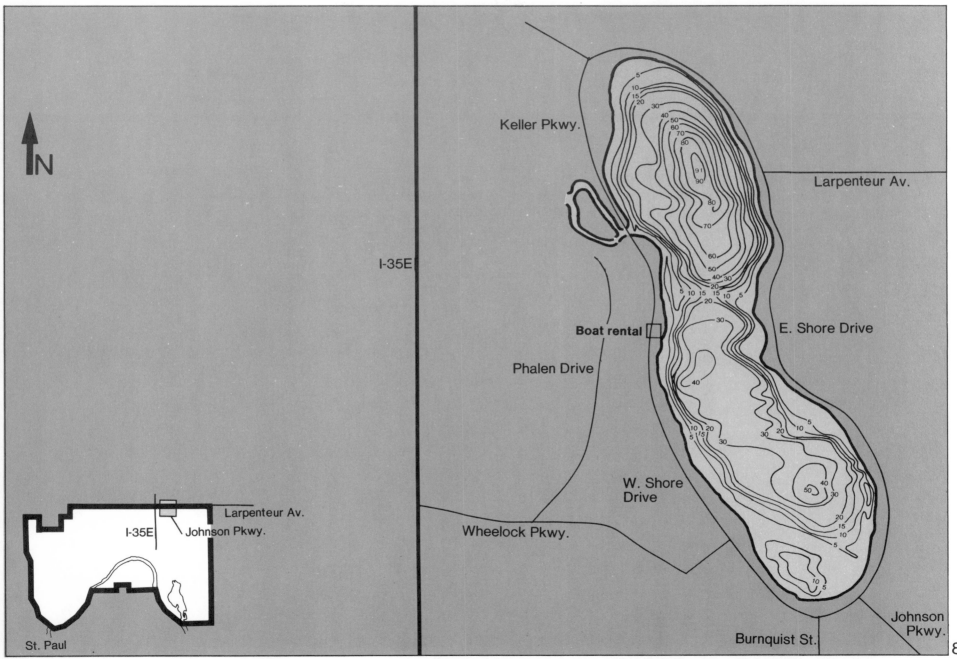

N

I-35E

Keller Pkwy.

Larpenteur Av.

Boat rental

E. Shore Drive

Phalen Drive

W. Shore Drive

Wheelock Pkwy.

Burnquist St.

Johnson Pkwy.

Larpenteur Av.

I-35E

Johnson Pkwy.

St. Paul

Prior Lake/

Size/
1,345 acres
Maximum depth/
50 feet
Water clarity/
poor

Gamefish present/
largemouth bass	perch
walleye	bullhead
bluegill	
crappie	
northern pike	

Public access/
southwest shore
Fee access/
Lakeside Marina (near Wagon Bridge),
Freddie's On The Lake (southwest shore).
Boat rental/
Lakeside Marina, phone 447-4300

Prior Lake fishing tips/

One of the better all-around fishing lakes in the Twin Cities. Heavily stocked with walleyes and northern pike by DNR. Crappie and bluegill fishing can be excellent, particularly in the winter. Prior Lake long has been a favorite with largemouth bass fishermen because of its history of producing whopper-sized "hawgs." Best producing spots are underwater points, weedy bays and rocky reefs.

Fisherman's advisory/
The lake is popular with speed boaters on weekends. Public launch has limited trailer parking space.

Prior Lake/

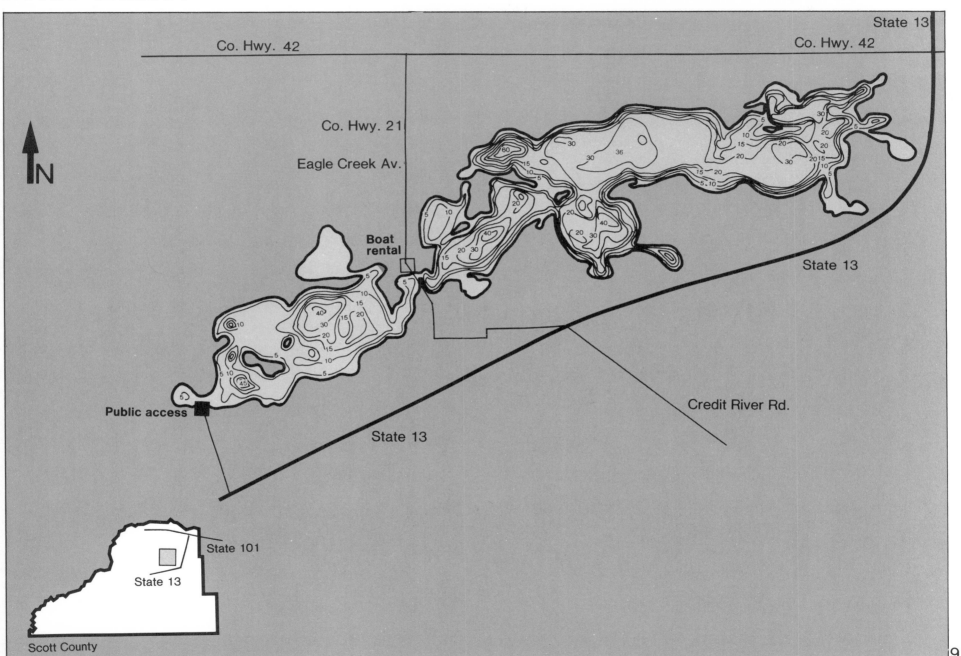

State 13

Co. Hwy. 42

Co. Hwy. 42

State 13

Co. Hwy. 21

Eagle Creek Av.

N

Boat rental

State 13

Credit River Rd.

Public access

State 13

State 101

State 13

Scott County

Big Carnelian Lake/

Size/
384 acres
Maximum depth/
70 feet
Water clarity/
good

Gamefish present/
largemouth bass	walleye
northern pike	perch
crappie	
bluegill	
bullhead	

Public access/
west shore
Fee access/
Greg's Place (west shore)
Boat rentals/
Oswald Resort (west shore), phone 439-3456;
Greg's Place (west shore), phone 439-8255

Big Carnelian fishing tips/

A most interesting fishing lake. High water levels have produced flooded timber and even flooded homes, giving Big Carnelian a variety of fishy-looking spots. The lake has excellent underwater weedbeds for northern pike and bass fishing. Pike population is high; bass run good sizes. Bluegills are abundant but small. Crappies may go up to one pound or better. Only a few walleyes are caught but most are big. Best spots are points, underwater weedline and flooded timbers.

Big Carnelian Lake/

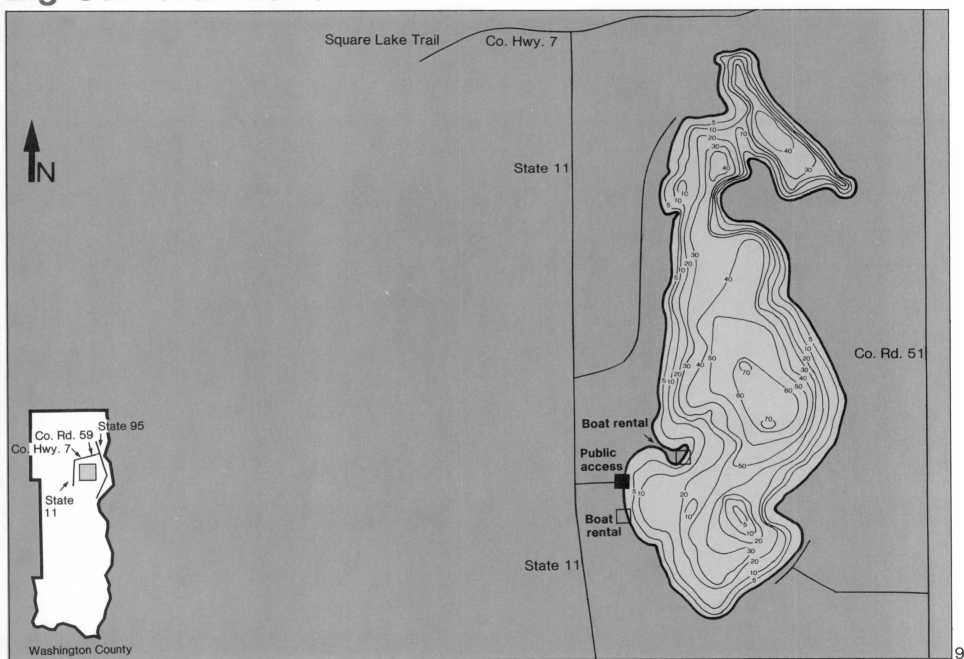

Square Lake Trail   Co. Hwy. 7

State 11

Co. Rd. 51

N

Boat rental

Public access

Boat rental

State 11

State 95
Co. Rd. 59
Co. Hwy. 7
State 11

Washington County

93

Big Marine Lake/

Size/
1,582 acres
Maximum depth/
60 feet
Water clarity/
good

Gamefish present/
northern pike   perch
largemouth bass   bullhead
walleye
crappie
bluegill

Public access/
north shore
Fee access/
Shady Birch Resort (southwest shore);
Veterans Rest Camp (southwest shore)
Boat rental/
Shady Birch Resort, phone 433-3391.

Big Marine fishing tips/

If you can't catch what you're after in Big Marine, they're not biting. The lake has lunker northern pike, walleyes and even bullheads. Big Marine's water levels are high, creating a variety of fish habitat. Weedlines, flooded flats and flooded timber are best for pike and bass. Bluegills and crappies are abundant but average size is small. The walleye count is not big but the size usually is.

Fisherman's advisory/
Public boat launch is shallow.

Big Marine Lake/

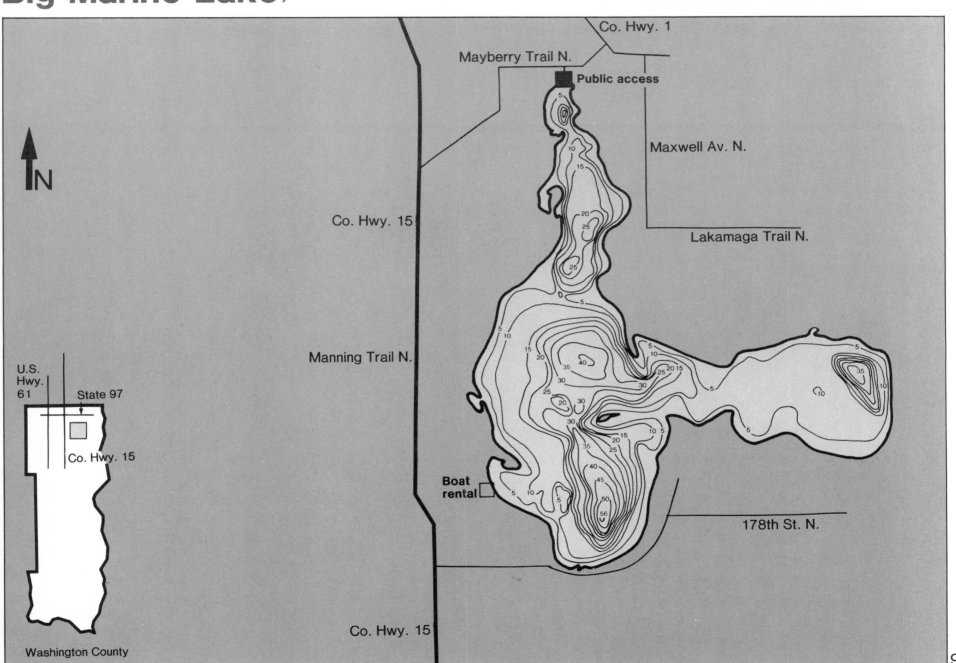

N

U.S. Hwy. 61

State 97

Co. Hwy. 15

Washington County

Co. Hwy. 15

Manning Trail N.

Co. Hwy. 1

Mayberry Trail N.

Public access

Maxwell Av. N.

Lakamaga Trail N.

Boat rental

178th St. N.

Co. Hwy. 15

Lake Elmo /

Size /
283 acres
Maximum depth /
127 feet
Water clarity /
fair

Gamefish present /
largemouth bass   perch
northern pike   bullhead
walleye
crappie
bluegill

Public access /
none
Fee access /
Pierre's Pier (east shore)
Boat rental /
Pierre's Pier, phone 770-0094 or 777-1642

Lake Elmo fishing tips /

Another fine all-around fishing lake for whatever your hook desires. Northern pike and largemouth bass counts are excellent. Troll or cast the weedline for best results. Bass will go to five pounds or better. Bluegill fishing is excellent and size is good. Crappie action is fair. Walleye catches are rare but fish tend to run large.

Fisherman's advisory /
If you intend to fish and waterski, forget it. Owners of the fee launch will not allow launching for waterskiing.

Lake Elmo /

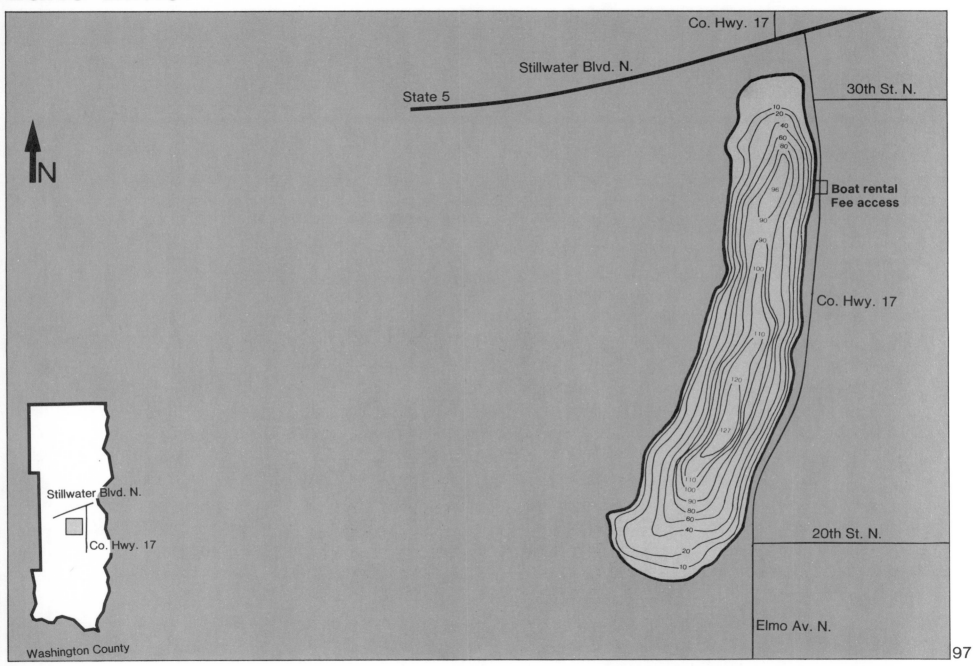

Co. Hwy. 17

Stillwater Blvd. N.

State 5

30th St. N.

10
20
40
60
80

96

90

90

100

110

120

127

110
100
90
80
60
40

20

10

Boat rental
Fee access

Co. Hwy. 17

20th St. N.

Elmo Av. N.

Stillwater Blvd. N.

Co. Hwy. 17

Washington County

Forest Lake/

Size/
2,251 acres
Maximum depth/
37 feet
Water clarity/
fair

Gamefish present/

walleye	rock bass
largemouth bass	bullhead
northern pike	
bluegill	
crappie	
perch	

Public access/
west shore, north shore
Fee access/
Tim's Marina, Willow Point Resort
Boat rental/
Tim's Marina, phone 464-9965;
Willow Point Resort, 464-2213

Forest Lake fishing tips/

The lake's many points and sunken islands will pay off to the angler who finds them. Expect action from northern pike and largemouth bass. The northern pike population is high. Expect a few lunkers. Panfishing for bluegills and crappies also can be good along drop-offs and weedbeds. Populations of both panfish species is high. The lake is popular with winter anglers.

Fisherman's advisory/
Forest Lake actually consists of three different lakes, each separated by narrows. Local fishermen often refer to the lakes as "Lake One," "Two" or "Three."

Forest Lake/

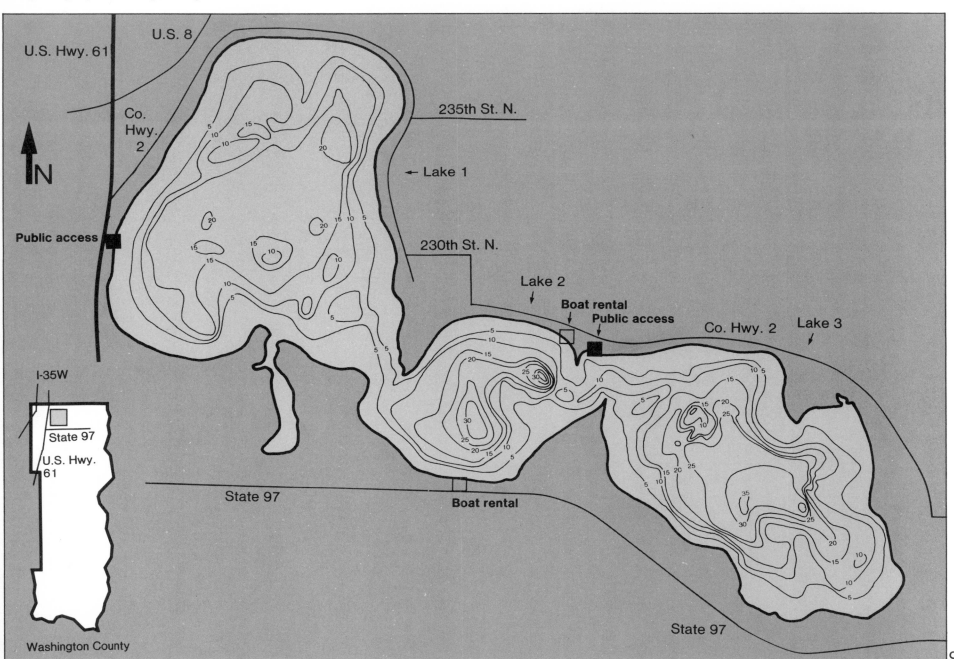

U.S. Hwy. 61

U.S. 8

Co. Hwy. 2

235th St. N.

N

← Lake 1

Public access

230th St. N.

Lake 2

Boat rental
Public access

Co. Hwy. 2

Lake 3

I-35W

State 97

U.S. Hwy. 61

State 97

Boat rental

State 97

Washington County

Jane Lake/

Size/
158 acres
Maximum depth/
30 feet
Water clarity/
excellent

Gamefish present/

northern pike	perch
largemouth bass	bullhead
bluegill	
crappie	
walleye	

Public access/
southeast shore
Fee access/
none
Boat rental/
none

Jane Lake fishing tips/

A fairly simple lake to fish because most of the action will be found along the underwater weedline. And it can be fast action. Jane Lake has high populations of northern pike and bass. The bluegills are abundant but small; the crappies will be keepers, although difficult to find sometimes. Jane also could be another sleeper for the bass angler looking for a lunker hole. A few walleyes swim in Jane but are seldom caught. DNR even found one sauger in the lake once. How it got there nobody knows. But, for sure, don't go to Jane intending to catch sauger.

Jane Lake/

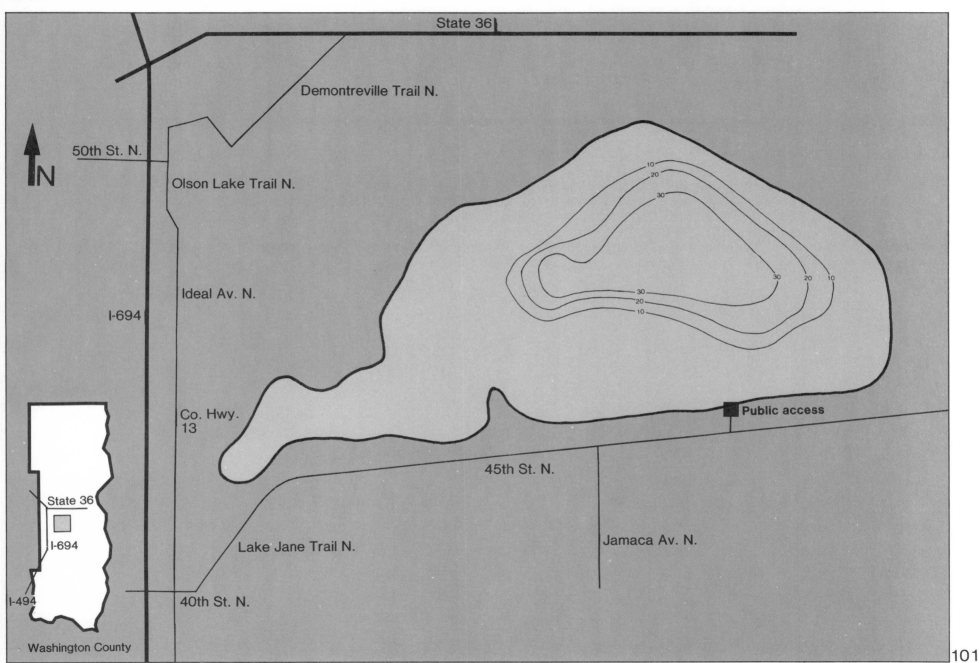

State 36

Demontreville Trail N.

50th St. N.

N

Olson Lake Trail N.

Ideal Av. N.

I-694

10
20
30

30
20
10

Co. Hwy.
13

30
20
10

Public access

45th St. N.

Jamaca Av. N.

State 36

I-694

Lake Jane Trail N.

I-494

40th St. N.

Washington County

Square Lake/

Size/
195 acres
Maximum depth/
68 feet
Water clarity/
excellent

Gamefish present/
brown trout   crappie
rainbow trout   bullhead
northern pike
largemouth bass
bluegill

Public access/
east shore
Fee access/
Golden Acres Campground (east shore)
Boat rental/
Golden Acres Campground, phone 439-9992 or 439-1147.

Square Lake fishing tips/

Square Lake is popular with scuba divers because it is the clearest lake in the metro region. More importantly, the divers will confirm that Square has mighty big brown trout up to 10 pounds or better. Rainbow trout also have been stocked but the sizes are smaller. Troll spoons or spinners for best results. Live bait will also take trout. But if the trout aren't biting, Square also has a good population of nice bluegills. Crappies are large but scarce. The largemouth bass and northern pike tend to run small size. But when there are lunker browns to be caught, who cares?

Square Lake/

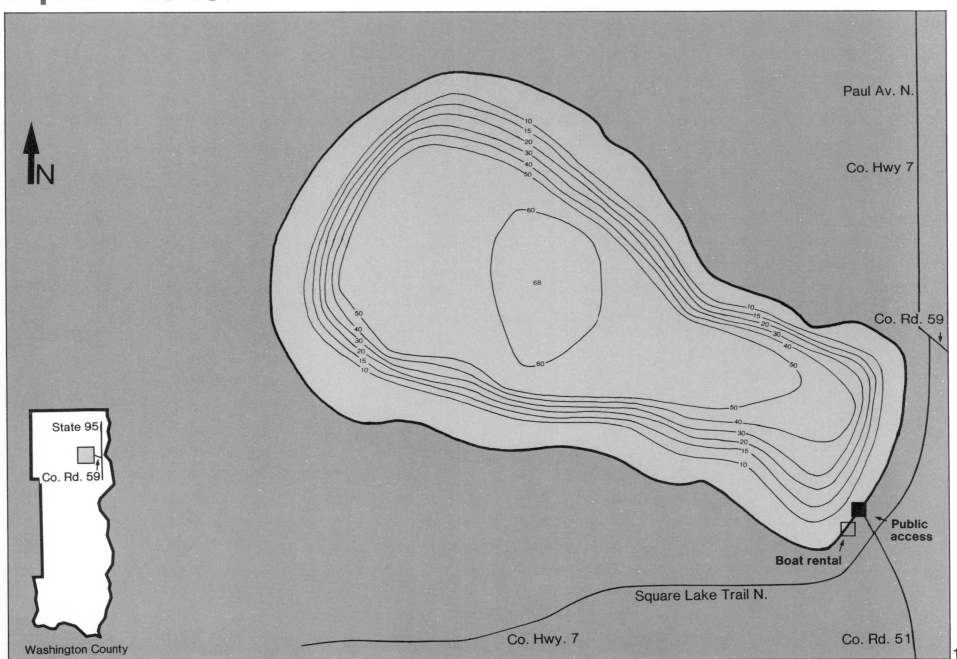

N

Paul Av. N.

Co. Hwy 7

Co. Rd. 59

10
15
20
30
40
50

60

68

50
40
30
20
15
10

60

10
15
20
30
40
50

50
40
30
20
15
10

State 95

Co. Rd. 59

Public access

Boat rental

Square Lake Trail N.

Co. Hwy. 7

Co. Rd. 51

Washington County

White Bear Lake /

Size /
2,416 acres
Maximum depth /
83 feet
Water clarity /
excellent

Gamefish present /
smallmouth bass   bluegill
walleye   crappie
largemouth bass   bullhead
perch
northern pike
rock bass

Public access /
northwest shore of North Bay

Fee access /
Spiess Landing (formerly Matoska Park), VFW Launch, Johnson Boat Works, White Bear Docking
Boat rental /
Tally's, (west shore), phone 429-2633

White Bear Lake fishing tips /

A super-clear lake that can be tough fishing except early and late in the day. But then the fishing can be super, particularly for walleyes. Look for the walleyes on rocky reefs and points. Smallmouth bass also will use the same haunts. Live bait will work best for smallmouth and walleye. Bluegill and pike tend to run small size. The crappie count is low. For lunkers, try for smallmouth and largemouth bass and walleyes. Muskies were stocked in 1975 but seem to have disappeared.

White Bear Lake/

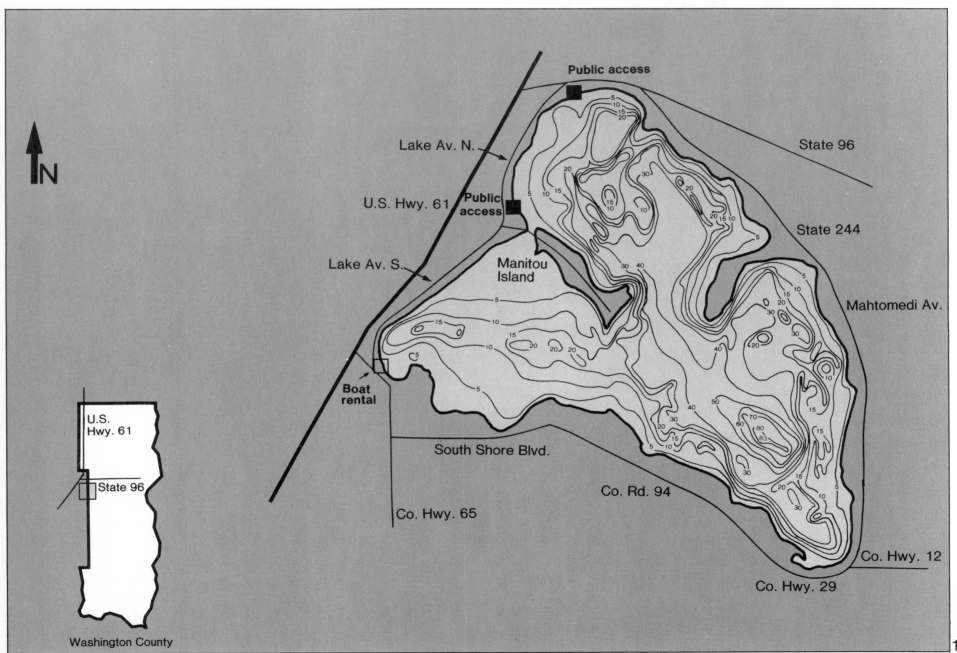

Public access

State 96

Lake Av. N.

U.S. Hwy. 61 — **Public access**

State 244

Lake Av. S.

Manitou Island

Mahtomedi Av.

Boat rental

South Shore Blvd.

Co. Rd. 94

Co. Hwy. 65

Co. Hwy. 12

Co. Hwy. 29

U.S. Hwy. 61

State 96

Washington County

St. Croix River /

Length /
25 river miles from Stillwater to mouth
Average depth /
9-foot channel maintained
Water clarity /
fair

Gamefish present /

walleye	channel catfish
sauger	bullhead
smallmouth bass	northern pike
largemouth bass	muskies
crappie	
white bass	

Public access /
near Alan S. King power plant south of Stillwater
Fee access /
Muller Boat Works, Stillwater; Bayport Park, Bayport; King's Marina, Hudson, Wis.; Beanie's Resort, south of Hwy.
12 bridge; Windmill Bill's Marina, Afton; Prescott Marine, Prescott, Wis.; Hastings Marine, Hastings
Boat rentals /
Beanie's Resort, south of Hwy. 12 bridge, phone 436-8874.

St. Croix River fishing tips /

A river must be "read" to produce good angling. The St. Croix is no different. Look for wingdams, rocky shores, eddies, deep holes, land points, sandbars. These are the river's fish haunts. Smallmouth bass nearly always are found next to rocky river habitat. The walleyes and sauger will be found near the wingdams, sandbars and rock banks near current. Catfish roam amid the eddies around log jams and in the deep river holes. The popular white bass also swim near the wingdams, sandbars and land points. Live baits, such as minnows and nightcrawlers, will produce the best river action. However, smallmouth and white bass will eagerly chase spinners and small jigs. White or yellow fluorescent jigs may be the best colors to try.

Fisherman's advisory /
Early- and late-season angling is best; extremely heavy boating crowds on weekends in midsummer.

St. Croix River/

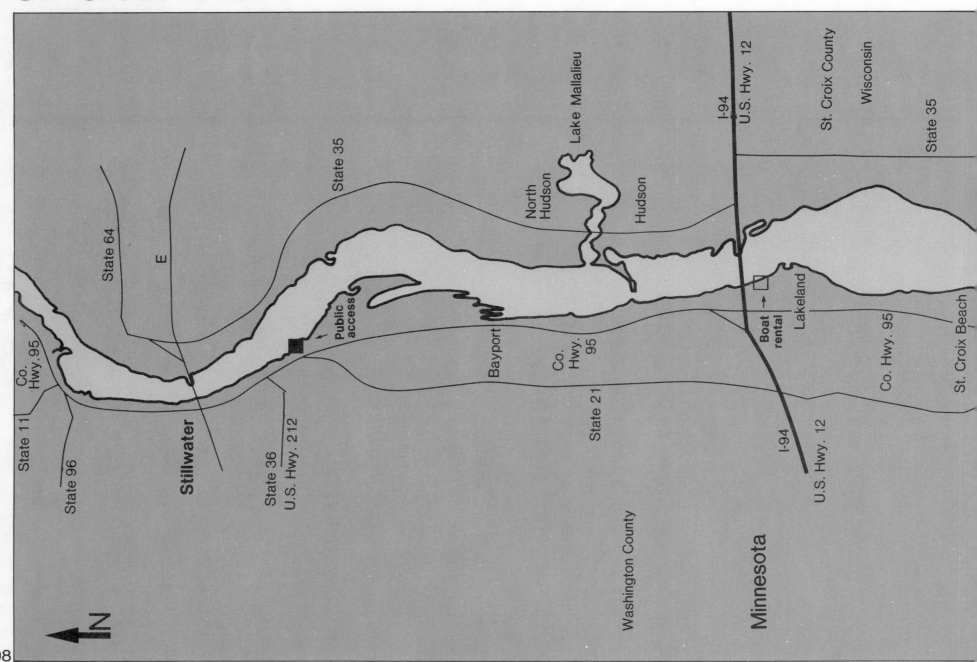

N

Stillwater

Public access

Bayport

North Hudson

Hudson

Lake Mallalieu

Lakeland

Boat rental

State 64

State 35

E

State 35

I-94

U.S. Hwy. 12

St. Croix County

Wisconsin

State 35

State 11

Co. Hwy. 95

State 96

State 36
U.S. Hwy. 212

State 21

Co. Hwy. 95

Co. Hwy. 95

St. Croix Beach

Washington County

Minnesota

U.S. Hwy. 12

I-94

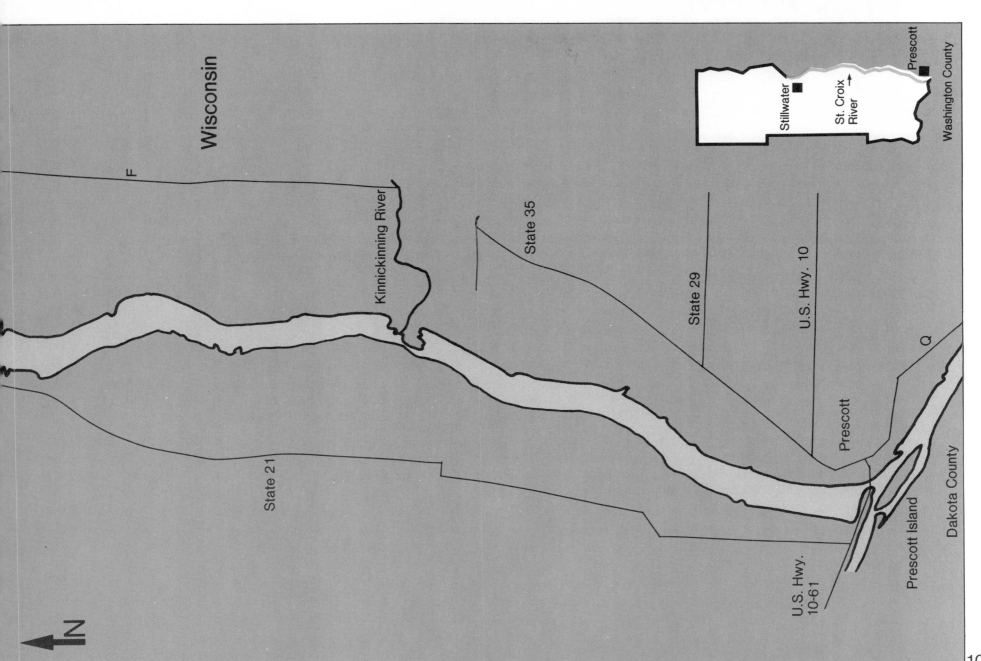

Wisconsin

F

Kinnickinning River

State 35

State 29

U.S. Hwy. 10

State 21

Prescott

U.S. Hwy. 10-61

Q

Prescott Island

Dakota County

N

Stillwater

St. Croix River

Prescott

Washington County

Mississippi River/

Length/
Approx. 60 river miles from Anoka to Hastings
Average depth/
Approx. 9-foot channel maintained
Water clarity/
fair

Gamefish present/

walleyes	northern pike
sauger	flathead catfish
smallmouth bass	bullhead
largemouth bass	crappie
channel catfish	bluegill
white bass	

Public access/
Coon Rapids Dam Park, 3 miles upstream from I-694 bridge; Camden Boat Ramp, ½ block south of Camden Bridge; Hidden Falls, north of W. 7th St. Bridge, St. Paul; Fort Snelling State Park; Harriet Island Park, St. Paul; Lilydale Ramp, Lilydale
Fee access/
Champlin City Launch, south of Champlin Bridge; Svoboda Boat Docks, St. Paul; Watergate Marina, St. Paul; Pool and Yacht Club, St. Paul; Harriet Island Harbor, St. Paul; St. Paul Yacht Club, St. Paul; Jolly Rogers Marina, Inver Grove; Willie's Marina, St. Paul Park; Bud's Place, 8 miles upstream from Hastings; Sorg's Picnic Grounds, 6 miles upstream from Hastings; Hub's Bait House, Hastings; Hastings Marina, Hastings; King's Cove, Hastings
Boat rentals/
None

Mississippi River fishing tips/

Nearly every fish species that is catchable swims within the Mississippi as it wanders through the Twin Cities. Rocky areas from Champlin downstream to Nicollet Island to below the Lake Street bridge harbor feisty smallmouth bass. Walleyes and sauger roam near the sandbars and along the cuts and bends in the main channel. Catfish may be found throughout the river stretch. Look for largemouth amid the flooded stump fields below St. Paul. But you may expect to catch any fish species regardless of where you cast. That's the nature of river angling. Live baits are best, minnows and nightcrawlers. Best all-around lure may be a fluorescent jig tipped with a minnow.

Mississippi River/

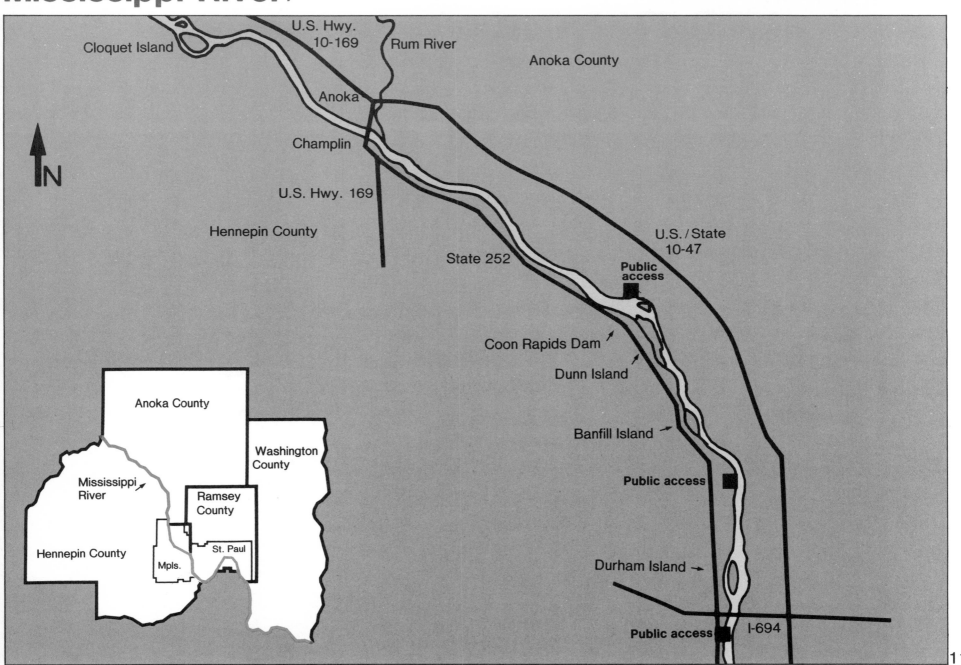

Cloquet Island

U.S. Hwy. 10-169

Rum River

Anoka County

N

Anoka

Champlin

U.S. Hwy. 169

Hennepin County

State 252

U.S. / State 10-47

Public access

Coon Rapids Dam

Dunn Island

Banfill Island

Public access

Durham Island →

Public access

I-694

Anoka County

Washington County

Mississippi River →

Ramsey County

Hennepin County

Mpls.

St. Paul

Mississippi River/

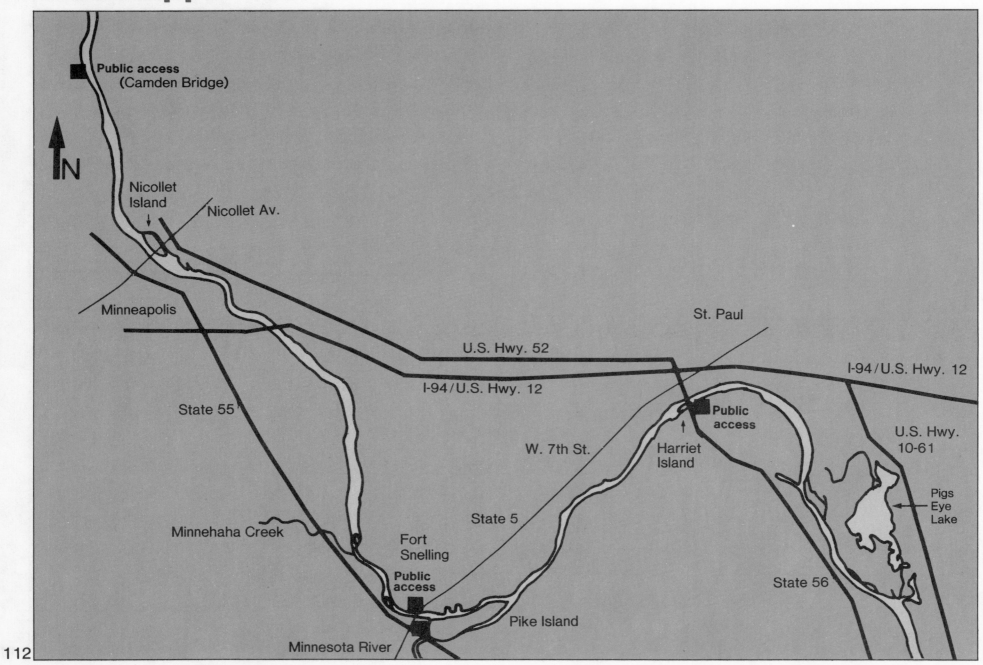

Public access
(Camden Bridge)

N

Nicollet
Island

Nicollet Av.

Minneapolis

St. Paul

U.S. Hwy. 52

I-94/U.S. Hwy. 12

I-94/U.S. Hwy. 12

State 55

**Public
access**

W. 7th St.

Harriet
Island

U.S. Hwy.
10-61

State 5

Pigs
Eye
Lake

Minnehaha Creek

Fort
Snelling

**Public
access**

Pike Island

State 56

Minnesota River

Mississippi River/

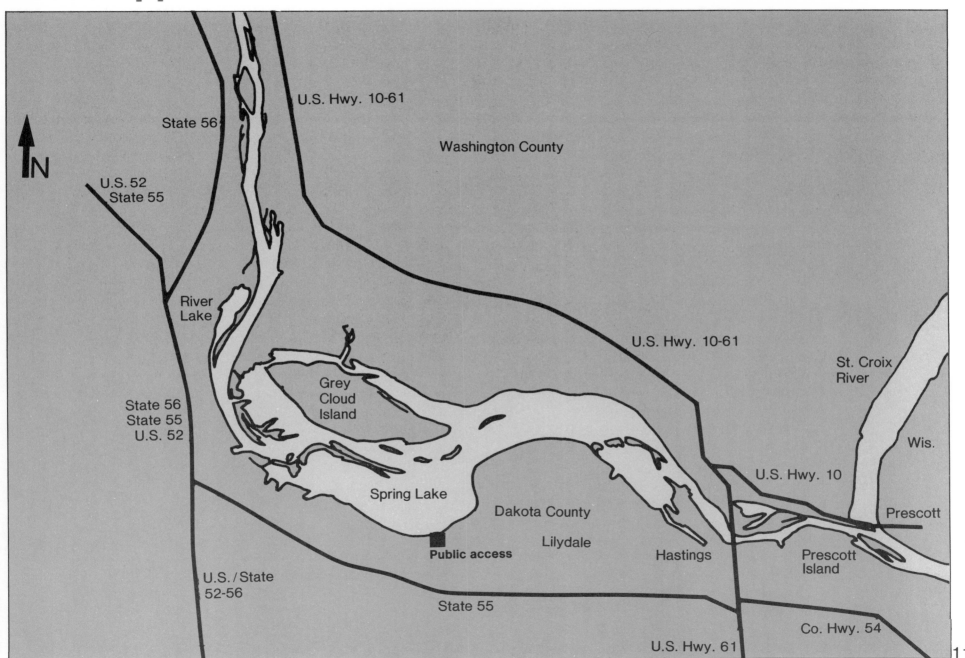

N

State 56

U.S. Hwy. 10-61

U.S. 52
State 55

Washington County

River
Lake

State 56
State 55
U.S. 52

U.S. Hwy. 10-61

St. Croix
River

Grey
Cloud
Island

Wis.

Spring Lake

U.S. Hwy. 10

Dakota County

Prescott

Public access

Lilydale

Hastings

Prescott
Island

U.S./State
52-56

State 55

Co. Hwy. 54

U.S. Hwy. 61

113

Rum River/

Length/
20 river miles from St. Francis to mouth at Anoka
Average depth/
varies, no maintained channel
Water clarity/
good

Gamefish present/
smallmouth bass
walleye
northern pike

Public access/
upstream near St. Francis; near Anoka State Hospital grounds, Anoka
Fee access/
none
Boat rental/
none

Rum River fishing tips/

An ideal river for float fishing from St. Francis to Anoka. Wading the river's riffles and pools also is easily done by gaining foot access at bridge crossings. But think of the Rum as the classic smallmouth bass stream. Go armed with small spinners, jig-spinner combos or small plugs. Remember: think small baits for smallmouth. The river's walleyes and northern pike will hit the same offerings, although those fish species are not as abundant as smallmouth. Fish the deep riffles and pools. Late summer bass fishing is best, particularly in the deeper river holes as the Rum enters Anoka. Float fishermen who want to continue onto the Mississippi River must portage to the right over the dam at Anoka.

Rum River/

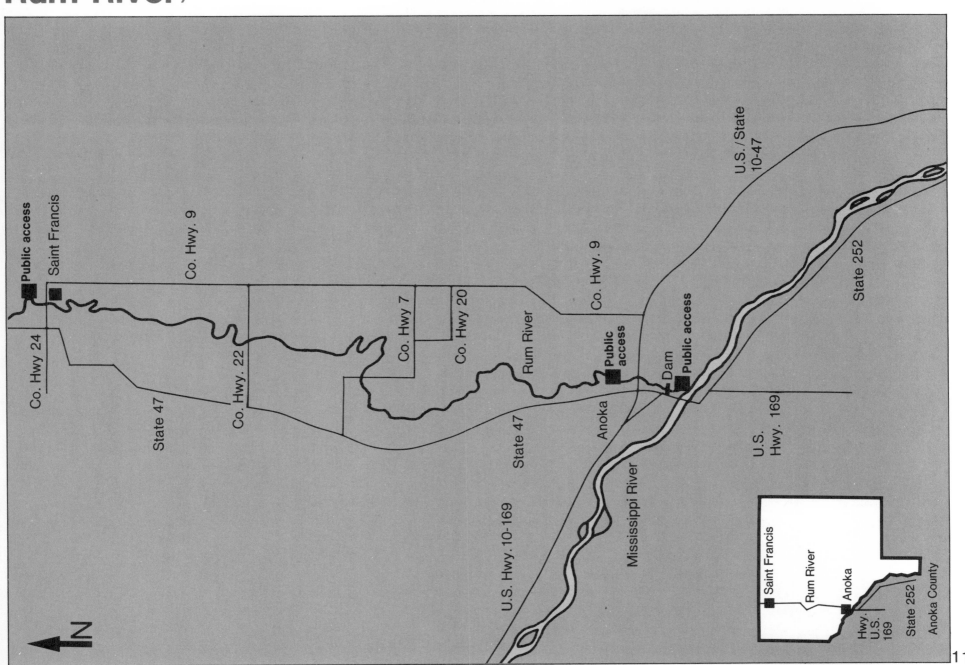

Public access

Saint Francis

Co. Hwy 24

State 47

Co. Hwy. 9

Co. Hwy. 22

Co. Hwy 7

Co. Hwy 20

Co. Hwy. 9

Rum River

State 47

Anoka

Public access

Dam

Public access

U.S./State 10-47

State 252

U.S. Hwy. 169

Mississippi River

U.S. Hwy. 10-169

N

Saint Francis

Rum River

Anoka

Hwy. U.S. 169

State 252

Anoka County

Other fishing places around town/

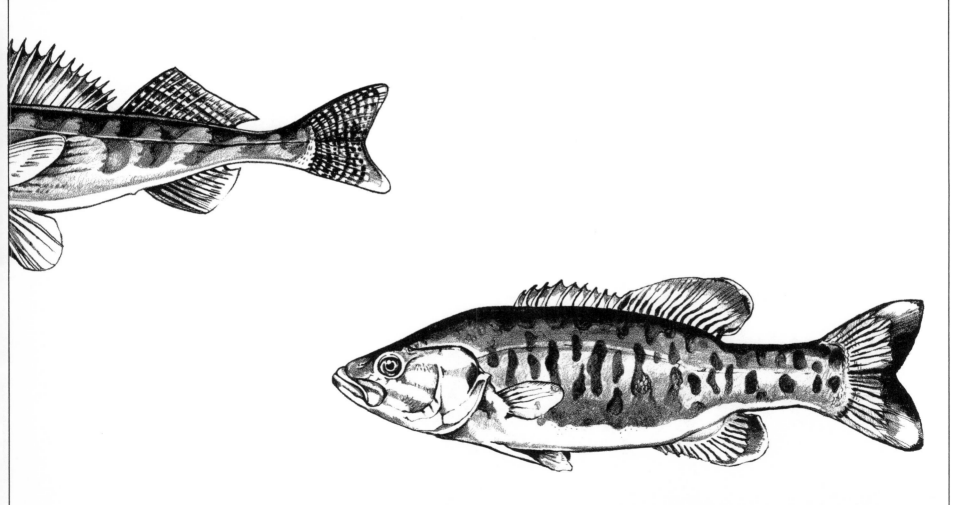

KEY: W=Walleyes   SMB=Smallmouth Bass   LKT=Lake Trout
      NP=Northern Pike   LMB=Largemouth Bass   BKT=Brook Trout
      C=Crappies   M=Muskies   RBT=Rainbow Trout
      B=Bluegills   CTF=Catfish   BRT=Brown Trout
      P=Perch   BLH=Bullheads

All lakes have public access unless otherwise noted.

Lake	Species of fish	Nearest town
Anoka County/		
Coon	C,NP,B,BLH	East Bethel
Crooked	B,C,LMB,NP,BLH	Coon Rapids
Ham	C,NP,LMB,B	Ham Lake
Moore	B,C,BLH	Fridley
Twin, East	B,C,NP	Elk River
Carver County/		
Auburn	NP,B,C	Victoria
Courthouse	RBT	Chaska
Eagle	LMB,B,NP	Young America
Hydes	C	Young America
Minnesota River	CTF,W	Chaska
Reitz	B,C	Waconia
Riley	B,C	Chanhassen
St. Joe	B,C	Chaska
Dakota County/		
Byllesby	W,B,CTF	Randolph
*Cannon River	SMB	Waterford
Crystal	LMB,NP,B	Burnsville
*Kennaleys Creek	BKT	Hastings
Minnesota River	CTF,W	Burnsville
Orchard	NP,B,C	Burnsville
*Vermillion River	CTF,W,B	Farmington
Hennepin County/		
Brownie	B,C	Minneapolis
Bryant	NP,B,C	Eden Prairie
†Christmas	NP,B,C	Chanhassen
*Crow River	SMB,W,B	Rockford
Crystal	NP,B,C	Robbinsdale
Fish	B,C	Maple Grove
Half Moon	B,C,BLH	Medina
Hiawatha	LMB,NP,B	Minneapolis
Long	BLH	Long Lake
Long, Little	B,C	Minnetrista
Minnesota River	CTF,W	Bloomington
Nokomis	NP,B,C	Minneapolis
Parkers	NP,BLH	Plymouth
Rebecca	LMB,CTF	Rockford
Sarah	LMB,NP,B,C	Rockford
Twin	NP,B,C	Robbinsdale
Whaletail	LMB,NP,B,C	Minnetrista
Wirth	B,NP	Minneapolis
Ramsey County/		
Como	B,C	St. Paul
Gervais	NP,B,C	Little Canada
Josephine	LMB,NP,B	Arden Hills
Keller	NP,B,C	Maplewood
Long	NP,B,C	New Brighton
McCarrons	B,C,BLH	Roseville
Owasso	LMB,NP,B,C	Roseville
Round	NP,B,C	Maplewood
Silver	W,LMB	North St. Paul
Silver	NP,B,BLH	Columbia Heights
Snail	LMB	Shoreview
Sucker	B,C	Vadnais Heights
Turtle	B,C	Shoreview
Vadnais	B,C	Vadnais Heights
Wabasso	LMB,B,C	Shoreview

Scott County/

Carls	LMB,W,B,C	Prior Lake
Cedar	W,LMB,B,BLH	New Prague
Eagle Creek	BRT	Savage
Fish	NP,B,C	Prior Lake
Minnesota River	CTF,SMB,W	Shakopee
O'Dowd	W,LMB,BLH	Shakopee
Shakopee Mill Pond	RBT	Shakopee
Spring	W,B,C	Prior Lake
Thole	BLH,B,C	Shakopee

Washington County/

Alice	B,C	Wm. O'Brien St. Park
Bone	NP,B,C	Forest Lake
*Browns Creek	BRT	Stillwater
Clear	W,B,C	Forest Lake
DeMontreville	BLH,B,C	Lake Elmo
Goose	BLH,B	Scandia
Lily	NP	Stillwater
Long	B,C	Mahtomedi
Sand	BLH	Marine
Tanners	NP,B,C	Landfall

* Lake has both public and private access.
† Private access only.